Ignite
Your Inner
Life Force

A Spiritual Introduction Guide for
Teenagers, Young Adults, Your True Self
and All Enlightened Seekers

KEVIN HUNTER

WARRIOR
OF **LIGHT**
PRESS
Los Angeles, California

Warrior of Light Press
www.kevin-hunter.com

Body, Mind & Spirit/Spiritualism
Inspiration & Personal Growth

Acknowledgements

This book is for you on your journey towards enlightenment. Thank you to my spiritual posse that includes, Luke, Veronica, Matthew, Enoch, Jacob, Samuel, Jeremiah and Saint Nathaniel. Thank you also to Archangel Michael and Archangel Gabriel.

CHAPTERS

Ignite Your Inner Life Force

Introduction

$\mathcal{I}$ often pay attention to others concerns in their life as it assists me in addressing those issues in a book at a later date. This is especially the case if it's a common issue. This way the information is always available and accessible for anyone who chooses to seek it out for eons to come.

When I say, 'we', I'm referring to my Spirit team of Guides and Angels in Heaven and I. The messages and guidance they filter through me come in primarily through my Clairaudience and Claircognizance channels. I'm the conduit in translating what they're giving me to put into a book in order to teach others who are guided to the information at any particular time in their life.

In, *Ignite Your Inner Life Force*, my Spirit team and I pass along some of the spiritual basics that have helped me along my often rocky and tumultuous journey. This is in order to assist you along your life path, whether you're new to spirituality or you enjoy picking up on different points of view. This is infused with practical messages, guidance, and answers that my Spirit team has taught and shared with me in order to impart it to those guided to it.

The main goal of all the *Warrior of Light* books is to assist in fine tuning your body, mind, and soul in order to expand your life and improve humanity one person at a time. You are a Divine communicator and perfectly adjusted and capable of receiving messages from Heaven on your own. This is for your benefit in order to help you live a happier and richer life. It is your individual responsibility to respect yourself and this planet while on your journey here. It does not matter who you are or what your interests are. You are loved regardless if others have told you otherwise.

The messages and information enclosed in this book may be in my own words, but they do not come from me. They come from God, the Holy Spirit, my Spirit team of guides, angels, and sometimes certain Archangels and Saints. I am merely the liaison or messenger in delivering and interpreting the intentions of what they wish to communicate. Often the information is a reminder for myself as well too!

I am one with the Holy Spirit and have many Spirit Guides and Angels around me. As my connections to the other side grew to be daily over the course of my life, more of them joined in behind the others. I have seen, sensed, heard, and been aware of the dozens of magnificent lights that crowd around me on occasion.

If I use the word "He" when pertaining to God, this does not mean that I am advocating that he is a male.

Simply replace the word, "He" with one you are comfortable using to identify God for you to be. This goes for any gender I use as examples.

The purpose of this book is to empower and help you improve yourself, your life, and humanity as a whole. It does not matter if you are a beginner or well versed in the subject matter. There may be something that reminds you of something you already know or something that you were unaware of. We all have much to share with one another, as we are all one in the end. This book contains information to help you reach the place where you can be a fine tuned instrument to receive your own messages from your own Spirit team. There may be a few places where I list another book of mine that surrounds a specific topic. This isn't to plug my work, but it's to direct readers who desire additional information on a topic they read about in this one. It's unrealistic and impossible to jam it all into one book.

Some of my personal stories may be infused and sprinkled throughout this book. This is in order for you to see how it has worked effectively for me. With some of my methods, I hope that you gain insight, knowledge, reminders, or inspiration. It may prompt you to recall incidents where you were receiving heavenly messages in your own life. There are helpful ways that can improve your existence and have a stronger connection with God and Heaven throughout this book. Doing so will greatly transform yourself in ways that allow you to attract wonderful circumstances at higher levels and live a happier more content life.

~Kevin Hunter

Spirit Guides and Angels

Your life force is the positive energy that flows through your soul. When it is operating at its highest state, then that is when you are most connected to God. When your life force energy drops, then this affects your mind and your physical body. This is followed by you experiencing a perpetual negative state such as always getting sick, depression, or permanent stress that never lightens. You lose interest in activities that once made you smile.

When your life force dwindles and remains permanently low, then it's time to ignite it. Igniting it will unleash any pent up repression that might have been forced upon you at the hands of others or at your own doing. You are not moving through your life alone. You are surrounded by heavenly helpers that are with you and within reach.

Every soul without exception who is living a human Earthly life has one Spirit Guide and one Guardian Angel who is with them from their human birth until their human death. This is regardless if you're aware of it or not, or whether you feel you are deserving of it.

Your Guardian Angel is a spirit being who has always resided in Heaven and never lived a life as a human soul, whereas your Spirit Guide has lived at least one Earthly life. More often than not your Spirit Guide is someone who is related to you. They can be a relative of yours from centuries ago or one who passed on not long before you were born. They go through formal training in Heaven before they can efficiently be allowed to guide an Earthly soul. One of the basic training rules given is they are not allowed to interfere with your free will choice unless it's to prevent your potential death before your time.

You might have more than one guide or angel if you are working with the other side and Heaven regularly. If you are involved in a life purpose activity that is geared towards assisting yourself or others on the planet in a positive way, then you may have more than one guide. Guides and Angels are also drawn to someone who displays love, joy, or peace traits on a regular basis. It can be someone who is innately a compassionate loving human being who does their best to do the right thing. This brightens that soul's light, which spirits see and feel. The guide or angel will come into that human soul's vicinity by being attracted to their light like a magnet.

If someone prays and communicates with God regularly, or works with spirit beings in Heaven, then they also tend to attract in other heavenly helpers to their side. These Guides and Angels might come into your space to begin the process of working with you in order to help you achieve a specific desire, pending that it is aligned with your higher self. They might come into your vicinity to work on easing your heart of sadness, anxiety, or stress brought upon by Earthly concerns and circumstances. You wake up one morning to discover that you're feeling quite good after experiencing a hard time. This is your Guardian Angel working on your spirit. You log onto the Internet and see an invitation to an event. You feel nudged to go to this event and while there you come into contact with someone who becomes your love partner for life. This is your Spirit Guide working with you.

Your personal Spirit Guide and Guardian Angel will be among the mix of souls on the other side that greet you when you cross over and head back home. Some have referred to your team as your invisible helpers, but this is not entirely accurate since your Guide and Angel are not invisible. They might be hidden to the naked eye for many, but they are most definitely visible in reality.

If you're someone with a highly calibrated Clair channel such as clairvoyance, clairaudience, clairsentience, claircognizance and so on, then you're more apt to being aware of your Spirit team. In fact, your team takes the form and shape that they know is familiar or comfortable for your human mind to process.

Others have been sharing their personal experiences and encounters with angels for centuries in all corners of the globe. The angels appear for that person just when they needed it most. Sometimes the angels materialize as a reminder to let you know they are indeed real and present for you. The angels and Archangels are God's hands and arms. They are an extension of Him. When you communicate with an angel, you are communicating with God. You are not praying to the angels, since all exaltation goes to God. Since it's difficult for a human soul to reach God, the angels are His gift to you in order to help you improve and raise your vibration so that your connection with Him is stronger. He is always communicating with you, but you do not pick up on that when experiencing any negative feelings. This is where the angels come in to lift you up so that you have a crystal clear communication line with God.

My mother recalled a story when I was eight years old. We were walking through a mall making our way through one of the shops and I was lagging behind her out of curiosity. She noticed I stopped to study the statue figures of angels on a shelf. She watched me concerned because the look on my face was one of anger, as if someone had provoked me. I looked at her astonished and said with irritation, "Why are they all blonde with wings? That's not how they look."

Not all spirit beings have wings, and this includes angels, even though artists have been depicting angels with wings for eons. This is due to the light of the angel being so bright that it seems as if there are wings behind them. Angels appear how they want to for that specific person. Sometimes they appear as a human being that shows up to help you in some way, and then they vanish without a trace. Most angels typically appear as white and/or blue sparkling lights. They are androgynous and are not in a human physical form, even though they may appear that way to ease the human mind.

Human soul's Guides and Angels reside in the dimension above the Earth's plane. It is easier to connect to them than if they were in one of the higher dimensions. Your Spirit team can see, hear, and feel you through this domain, but you will have a tougher time connecting with them in return due to the heavy density wall that separates these worlds. It's kind of like the movie, "Hunger Games", but only the part where the Capitol President and its people are able to see those fighting in the Hunger Games arena. Those in the arena are unable to see those watching them. This is a generalized description since this is also where the comparison ends. This is merely to establish a visual of what it's like between you and your Spirit team.

There were episodes in the series, "True Blood" that showcased a doorway into a fictionalized world where Fairies resided. The doorway and transporting part of that design was not far off from the transition of dimensions such as the Earth sphere to the next dimension where Heaven and the Realm world exist. Another Science Fiction piece that is also not far off in describing the planes is the "Twilight Zone". The logline of that series basically says that the twilight zone is the doorway into another dimension. The creators of these entertainment pieces and most Science Fiction entertainment come from the Realm of the Star Person (a.k.a. Star Child, Star Seed, Star Soul). They might not have been aware that they were receiving these visions, ideas, and information from above. Regardless, they've incorporated them into the entertainment part of human reality. This information they receive is dropped into the deepest part of their subconscious. This subconscious space is where the connection with the other side resides.

You are a spirit whose life force never dies, even if it feels that way sometimes. Your spirit resides in a temporary physical body in order to have an Earthly life for a variety of purposes. The body you inhabit will not last forever. It will age and eventually give out. In the human reality, you call it a death, but it is not a death as your spirit is still intact and very much alive. It is just no longer crammed and stuck in its human physical body that weighs you down. Your physical body is a rental and you want to take care of this rental with good diet and exercise.

In the spiritual genre, many use the terminology, "Body, Mind and Soul". Those affiliated with that genre have the goal of improving all aspects and the totality of one self. This is by loving your body and taking care of it, but also by being aware that you have a soul that you need to take care of as well. You want to be aware and in tune to the idea of who and what you are. When your physical body has given out and is no longer functioning, then your soul exits its body and passes through a tunnel of light to the other side. This other side as some call it is reached by moving through the doorway or tunnel of light into another dimension.

This other dimension is where Heaven and other dimensions exist.

More often than not, you agreed to have a physical life for a variety of purposes. Everyone is on the planet with the goal of spreading the three biggest traits aligned with God: Love, joy, and peace. All words affiliated with those three words describe what Heaven is like. You may look around and wonder how humanity grew to be removed from those phenomenal traits, but it is the reason you are here. Life is rough for some and reaching that state of being can be challenging, but it is not impossible.

I have many books geared towards the improvement of humanity, which in the end is having the goal of taking you, others, and the life that you have at this moment seriously. You do not want to forget to have fun and inject joy into your life as well. Heaven cares about humanity and has been displeased with how everyone treats one another on Earth, not to mention the crises state the planet is in. This is from the environment, to the unnecessary destruction of nature, animals, and other people.

Building physical dwellings on top of one another has contributed to this suffocating feeling and disconnected others from God. It's a struggle to reach a true connection with tampering energies around you, but alas it's not unmanageable with practice. Some are nonchalant and in denial about the current state of Earth. They debunk the idea that anything is wrong with it. They write it off and take no responsibility in contributing to the damage of the world.

This might sound like some kind of science experiment gone wild placing you here to live an

Earthly life and then removing your memory of who and what you are. The truth is that your memory is not technically or completely erased. The Earth's density and the many blocks around you have limited the important parts of this memory. Past life memories are reduced to nothing unless it is relevant. Otherwise you'd be experiencing heavy emotion over something you did in a past life.

All souls have access to the deeper parts of their consciousness. When you are born, you are 100% psychic and in tune to all things around you, beyond, and on over to the other side. Gradually, your caregivers, peers, and the society you grew up in began to have a larger influence on your human development. They train you on what to like, what not to like, and how to think. The ones who break away from that cycle typically have incarnated from a realm on other side. They know they have an important mission or purpose here, even if it's to spread compassion, love, or joy to others in some manner.

The negative influences around you dimmed your connection and light to Heaven. How these contributors did this was by putting images in front of you of the physical world and inflicting the limited routines onto your way of life. This included that you're disciplined and on a schedule. You go to bed at a certain hour and you wake up around the same hour. You have breakfast and you head off to school, or when you're older you head to a job or a career. The school schedule is relatively the same and so is your job schedule. You drive back and forth to work to make money to pay for your car, a place to live, food, as well as clothing. You do this indefinitely while falling deeper into the routine of physical Earthly life, which is not the soul's true existence at all in the end.

If you do not feel you are in tune, then your first goal is to begin the process of becoming more in tune. This means paying attention to everything around you beyond the physical. The physical is anything that is manmade such as cars, phones, buildings, airplanes, the noise, the internet, social media, houses, your human body, someone else's body, your exterior, the drama and negativity created by others, and on and on. None of that is real or important in the end on your soul's journey. One thing that both believers and non-believers can agree upon is that one day this will all cease to exist for you. The human physical death is not the end.

Your Guide and Angel assist you along your Earthly life. They guide you down a path that benefits your higher self. Your higher self is all traits aligned with optimism such as love, joy, and peace. These are words that are also what Heaven is like while living there. Your lower self is your ego and sometimes considered the Devil, since there is no real Devil ruling a pit of fire somewhere to harm your soul for all eternity. The Devil is humankind behaving at their worst. It is aligned with the harm, hurt, and hate traits. It is the bully that seeks to destroy someone else because they are different. It is the part of you that wallows in any negative feeling or thought. This might be anger, stress, depression, sadness, or confusion. Someone who is a gossip and trash talks others resides in their lower self. The lower self is cut off from God and is not psychic, while the higher self is part of God and the Holy Spirit. Your higher self is 100% psychic and in tune with what resides beyond and outside of this physical existence.

Those who grow to be more in tune and who work with God and Heaven tend to have more Guides and Angels around them. Those who have big purposes in this life also attract in additional Guides and Angels to assist them in obtaining particular goals. Some of these Guides and Angels may permanently stay by your side throughout your life purpose guiding and assisting you.

The Archangels

The Archangels are hierarchy spirit beings that manage the angels and reside in another dimension. Like Guides and Angels, you can request the assistance of a specific Archangel to come into your life when needed. Many of them have traits they specialize in, such as Archangel Michael is God's General. He goes to battle for you, gives you strength, and protects you from harm. Archangel Raphael is the healing angel that can help with anything health or well-being related. He might assist by guiding you to exercise, change your diet, and find the right doctor, or healer. Archangel Gabriel helps the artists and parents of the world. She's the motivator pushing you to get to work on creative projects. She was also the one who delivered the news of Christ's birth. Archangel Uriel is the one who gives you those great light bulb ideas and shines a light on the path you're intended to be on. The Archangels are God's hands and arms as well. This means when you're communicating with an Archangel, you're immediately communing with God.

Archangels, angels, and spirit guides show up in your vicinity the minute you call out to them. The archangels, like the angles, are androgynous. This means they have no anatomy. They are referred to as a specific gender, and may even appear that way to some, because it is easier for human souls to relate to them this way.

I go into detail over sixteen of the thousands of Archangels that exist in my pocket book, *Connecting with the Archangels*.

Communicating With Heaven

When any spirit being in Heaven communicates with you, the tone is direct, full of love, and uplifting, even if they are warning you of danger. They communicate firmly, while your ego communicates with uncertainty, anger, or any other disapproving emotion. Your Spirit team will never advise you to do something that ends up hurting you or someone else. This can be something such as developing a sudden urge to recklessly pack up and move away all of a sudden. It can be leaving a soul mate connection that was intended for you in order to go after someone else. Notice around you whom it might hurt including yourself. Typically rash decisions tend to come from the ego since the ego is impatient. It believes the grass is always greener elsewhere, but where it currently is.

I've witnessed countless incidents where others have continuously made rash impulsive decisions that end up being regrettable to the person in the end. It takes them downward, rather than upward. Before they know it, years have passed and they're no closer to what they want than where they started. If you're involved with someone or have a family, then your team would never advise you to pack up and move. When you do that, you may find this choice you made doesn't go as planned. It delays you from achieving what you really want. You discover after the decision that it is not what you expected, or you end up losing the person that loved you more than any other. The more you work with your Spirit team, then the better you get at deciphering what is your Spirit team and your higher self, and what is your ego or lower self.

Your Spirit Guide, Guardian Angel, God, or any entity or spirit communicates with you through your senses. Your senses are not to be confused with your physical senses, but these senses are interwoven between your physical body and your soul. These senses are also referred to as *clairs*, which means 'clear'. It is being a clear channel with the other side. There are over a dozen clair points in your soul, but there are four primary clairs. Many have one or two dominate clairs, but those who work on opening up the other clairs have all four clair channels opened up and even some of the others. It takes work and a lifestyle change to keep them open since a clair can easily dim or close. Your clairs are also considered to be extra sensory perception, because the clair senses reach places beyond what your physical senses are able to do. You hear the voices of spirit, but your physical ears are not hearing them, it's your spirit/soul senses that hear them. The "extra sensory" part of the equation is the extra sense that is beyond the physical.

You have a telepathic hit when you are thinking of someone you haven't communicated with for a while, and then suddenly they contact you out of the blue to say they were thinking of you and wanted to reach out. You might say to them, "How weird, as I was just thinking about you recently."

Your Spirit team is implanting this information in your mind for a reason. Maybe it's to remind you of the good that existed in that person and how they made you feel. Perhaps it's to bring you both together again to resolve old issues and bring the connection to proper closure. Or it could be that you or this other person has information or wisdom that is passed onto you when you have that conversation. Sometimes it can simply be a good, positive, fun discussion that uplifts you out of a mood you've been in or you uplift them.

You both had a telepathic communication line flowing back and forth between your souls. Telepathy is what is unspoken, but soon proves to be true. Telepathy can be that someone is thinking of you and transmitting this information to you, which wakes you up to suddenly be thinking of them. Some say when you're thinking of someone that they are likely thinking of you. While this can certainly be true, typically one of you ends up reaching out to the other at some point not long afterwards. The telepathy has a measure of psychic foresight to it. You can also have telepathic communication with a soul on the other side, such as a departed loved one.

It is assumed that someone with psychic abilities is gifted, but these gifts have been given to every living soul. No one is more special than anyone else where psychic abilities are concerned. Everyone is psychic and has the ability to connect. Some connect easier than others or in different ways than someone else does. They might have worked to re-open their clair senses, or they live a life that has minimal blocks in their environment. All souls have psychic gifts, but you're not paying attention to this input of information if you are buried deeply in the physical world. This comes with an array of blocks that reduces your psychic gifts. The good news is that one's psychic gifts never go away. They might dim or darken, but they're accessible to anyone who chooses to re-awaken that part of their soul.

The Four Main clairs are Clairvoyance, Clairaudience, Clairsentience, and Claircognizance. Read the basic descriptions in the coming pages in this chapter in order to pinpoint what best describes you. You may feel that a description explains what you have, but then you may protest, "I don't have that clair."

The descriptions are the basics of how to recognize you or someone else as having that clair. Consider studying more up on a particular clair and how to develop and open it up. It's already there as it's a part of you, but it just needs to be worked out. It's the same way someone who goes to the gym regularly to build muscle. If they suddenly stopped going, the muscle would lessen over time. Clairs work in that same respect. You treat it like a muscle that needs to be built, strengthened, and taken care of. Your physical body can build muscle or tone when you exercise.

Your clair channels work in the same way. When you exercise a clair, then you build its muscle over time. From that point, you do the work out maintenance as you would if you were exercising regularly to strengthen your physical body and overall health.

Clairvoyance

Clairvoyance means "Clear Seeing" (or "Clear Vision"). You have clairvoyance if you receive visual images, cues, or impressions through your mind's eye. Your mind's eye is also called the *third eye*. The third eye looks like an eye and is located between your two physical eyes, but slightly raised above it. It cannot be seen with your physical eyes. If you close your eyes and focus on seeing your third eye, then you should be able to see it with practice. It is behind the area between where your eyes are located turned right side up. When you see violet light around the third eye area or in your peripheral vision, then your clairvoyance is opening up. Someone might be born into this lifetime blind through their physical eyes, yet they receive powerful psychic visual impressions through their third eye. The third eye is where your clairvoyance channel sees the messages and guidance ones Spirit team is communicating to them. Your Guides and Angels show you these messages through a moving picture like a movie, which later proves to be true.

Clairvoyant messages often need to be decoded. The reason is the communication is being brought to you through a moving visual picture or still image. The significance of the illustration does not always mean what is being shown to you. It is up to you to decipher what the message is supposed to be about. If you are someone who has vivid dreams, which you recall long after you've woken up from sleep, then this is a sign that you have clairvoyant abilities. If you find clairvoyance to be your strongest clair, then investigate on awakening this channel and cracking it open.

Here's an example of clairvoyance: You are asleep and having a dream where you are walking the streets at night. There are hundreds of snakes and cobras moving about around you attacking everyone except you. As a clairvoyant, it's your goal to decipher what this moving image means, because it's highly unlikely that this is an image showing you of what's to come. It can mean that you're a rising successful star in your profession who is untouchable, but this is not met without enemies. There is someone or many who are or will be jealous of you. This could be one way to interpret the dream of the snakes attacking everyone around except you.

You have clairvoyance if you also see spirits from the other side. It looks as if they're in front of you or to the side of you. They don't look like actual physical people, which is the way they're portrayed in some Hollywood films. They look more opaque or translucent. You may even see them as lights or sparkling lights in your peripheral vision. For some, your conscious will block your abilities to see spirits for fear of seeing a deceased spirit looking the way they had when they passed away. They might have died a violent death such as a murder or car accident. The spirit is fine and doesn't look like that on the other side, but they can appear how they choose to a human soul.

This sometimes includes how they looked when they died or the age they passed away. If they died a violent death, then they might appear that way to be recognizable to you. Someone's grandfather passed away at 92 years old, but when he crossed over he appears in top form looking like a young 25-34 year old human. He might appear 92 years old in human years to a psychic medium in order for that medium to relay what is coming through on a reading for someone. You might not know who the medium was talking about if your grandfather appeared the way he did at 25 years old. He would look significantly different if he appeared as he is on the other side.

Clairvoyant messages can come in the disguise of symbols, numbers, colors, letters, words, and pictures that have a meaning to you or someone else. It can be something from the past, the present, or future. Those who have clairvoyance have a tendency to daydream. These daydreams may be random or they may be images of what's happened, what's happening, or what's to come. They see their own future as if it's a vision board of what is to take place at some point. When someone tells a clairvoyant friend a story, the clairvoyant is living the story as if it's happening to them personally. They see the story as if they are the main character.

Clairsentience

Clairsentience means, "clear feeling", (or "clear sensation"). This is when you feel the messages, guidance and impressions coming in from Heaven.

Those who have high clairsentience might walk into a building and feel as if all eyes are on them. Or they will pick up on a sense of foreboding that tells them to get out of a particular place. They perceive danger is about to happen and then it soon does. They also intuit good stuff that is coming into their vicinity as well, which ends up happening. You might have a strong upbeat joyful feeling that the job you want is going to come about, and then this later proves true. Having clairsentience is when your Spirit team communicates messages and guidance through your feelings.

You might be the kind of person who becomes emotionally upset when someone you're interested in romantically is not reciprocating that interest. You text and email this person regularly hoping to illicit a response that is satisfying to you. Yet the object of your desire is casual in their reply when communicating with you, or they continuously drop the ball with your text dalliance. You question whether or not they're truly interested in you. When they throw you a bone and click 'like' on one of your social media posts, then you're suddenly on cloud nine believing they're interested in you. Soon you grow upset when a week has passed and you haven't heard from them. While repeatedly becoming emotionally upset over something like this comes from your ego, the emotional upset you're experiencing is a clairsentient message that this person is not as interested as you were hoping. They might be interested in you on some level, but not in the way you crave. To endure keeping this connection alive will only frustrate and depress you. When they give you a rare 'like' or comment on your social media page, or they text you, then this catapults you into feeling as if this person is deeply interested in you.

One should avoid engaging with someone who is seriously interested in you in a way that you are not with them. The reason is the person deeply interested in you sees any form of contact you make with them as a sign of interest. Even if the contact you make is telling the other person to stop contacting you. It doesn't matter since you're giving that person attention, whether it is good or bad, it's still attention and gets them going. This is why you cut that out cold turkey and do not respond or show interest to someone that you do not have deep feelings for, but you know they feel deeply for you. Pay attention to your feelings, as this is the accurate barometer gauge on what is real and what is not. When you move your ego out of the way, you're able to decipher the accuracy of Heaven's incoming messages through clairsentience.

Someone with clairsentience can be all over the place when it comes to feelings and emotions. You will want to ensure you work on well-being exercises that keep your emotional balance on an equal footing in order to communicate with Heaven efficiently. With clairvoyance, the clairvoyant will hear someone telling them a story, and will see the story as if it were a movie and actually happening to them. With clairsentience, the person listening to the story will 'feel' what's happening in the story as if it's happening to them. Sometimes if it's a horrific story, the clairsentient may say, "You have to stop." Because the feelings they're experiencing over the story are so overwhelming it's as if it's happening to them.

Gifted actors tend to have highly calibrated clair channels, which enable them to effectively inhabit a character as if they're walking in that person's shoes. In the media today, you see good-looking people attempting to become successful actors. They rarely experience success, because they only look good on the surface, but have clair channels that are not bouncing off the scale. This is why some will see movies or television shows with someone super good looking and find them to be lousy actors. They were hired for their looks and not their talent, since the entertainment industry knows that the public gets off on staring at some eye candy.

If you have heard others accuse you of always being too sensitive, then this is a clue that you may have a high degree of clairsentient gifts, which are ready to be awakened. When others find you too sensitive, it can be because every little thing that someone says or does bothers you. Your ego is unable to control your reaction. When you develop your clairsentience and understand how it works, how to shield yourself, then you react less to every shred that comes your way.

When you have clairsentience, you receive hunches and gut feelings about situations and circumstances. You hear a friend say, "I just had this gut feeling that I should've gone down this other road instead. I should've listened to it, otherwise this would not have happened." This is a sign that you're receiving guidance and messages from your Spirit team. Those with clairsentience absorb other people's energy like a sponge. They may find it difficult to be in overcrowded areas. They've complained that it's challenging standing in a grocery store line due to the heavy input of other people's energies. You can sense the emotions and feelings of others and know what feels wrong to you. This can be psychic overload, which is why those with strong clairsentience keep to themselves or stay away from crowds or large amounts of people as much as possible.

Clairsentient people feel every little nuance around them. At times this becomes uncomfortable and draining. This prompts them to take frequent breaks of alone time. They sense everything around them from people's emotions to what's to come for someone. Their internal feelings are all over the place like a roller coaster ride. They may give the illusion they are extremely put together on the outside, but on the inside they're wrestling with all sorts of uneasy emotions that constantly ebb and flow like the ocean. They are prone to being a bit jumpy as if someone moved quickly behind them. They turn around to find no one there. Clairsentient people are ridden with anxiety, nervousness, and have a fight or flight response to any and all around them. Imagine absorbing everyone else's feelings being poured into you and how that might make you feel.

A clairsentient being feels the answers, messages, and guidance filtering through them from Heaven. The way Heaven communicates with this person is through their feeling sense. Someone who senses something specific that has happened, is happening, or is going to happen is someone who has a strong clairsentient channel. They are super sensitive to every nuance around them. Those who have incarnated from the Realm of the Incarnated Angel tend to have a high degree of clairsentience.

Clairaudience

Clairaudience means "Clear Hearing" (or Clear Audio). When you're clairaudient you hear the voices of God and your Spirit team. You can differentiate between the voices of you and the voices of Heaven by its accuracy of the message being relayed. When you look back during the times you were in danger, you might recall when you received a heavenly message through that channel. When there is an urgent situation that could put you in danger, you may hear a voice shout, "Run!" And this gets you up and going. You later protest that if you didn't run who knows what might've happened.

I have strong clairaudience and I hear voices, words, and sounds coming in through one of my ears that later comes true. One of my ears is partially deaf. Ironically that is the ear that the messages come in the strongest as if it's loud and clear. I've been an avid music listener since I was a child, and I had dreams of being a rocker or musician. I could live without communicating in any form except through the sounds of music. I hear the words clearly from my Spirit team as I'm listening to the notes and chord changes in a song. The words of Spirit flow and interweave through these notes effortlessly. My clairaudience channel works much like an old radio where you're changing the station between the static to receive a clear station.

Every so often a ringing in my ear buzzes and it's a sound that hasn't been detected to be a medical issue. It's been like that my entire life. This buzzing is the sound of my Spirit team downloading important information into my consciousness that is discovered to be of importance at a later date. I've relayed messages to a stranger about someone who has passed on that they know. I've said their loved ones name as it is the name I hear through clairaudience. Hearing things about others through this channel is what has convinced me that there is more to this life than this plane. I'm communicating with someone on the other side who I do not know. The stranger I'm relaying the information to informs me that it's someone they knew who passed away.

There is no way I can know this information when it's a stranger, but they have confirmed that what I've told them is true. I hear the deceased person talking in my ear. They are not dead in the sense that one believes someone to be dead. They reside 'somewhere' and are very much alive and well. Having these occurrences happen sporadically throughout my life since I was old enough to construct sentences has convinced me that this is not the end. I may not be able to hand over the material physical concrete proof that a non-believer would desire, but I have proof enough for myself. Whether someone believes in it or not is their journey to face, while I have mine.

Those with higher ranges of clairaudience tend to be musicians and singers. They might not be aware of it, but they can certainly develop it. If someone's work is connected to sounds and music, then they hear guidance and messages through the notes of these sounds. Ludwig Van Beethoven composed some of the most memorable and beloved music in history, yet he was also considered deaf. This irony begged others to question, "How on Earth did he write these incredible pieces if he is deaf?" His hearing was faint, but spirit infused his clairaudience channel with music that has long been remembered over the centuries.

Other clairaudients may find that they mumble or talk to themselves, and yet they're perfectly sane. They find they're having conversations with spirit without realizing it or trying to. It's talking as if you talk to a friend on the phone. The conversations or talking isn't random and full of gibberish. It is clear concise information that later proves true, or is positively helpful to that person or another.

The voices a clairaudient hears through their "Ear Chakra" are not to be mistaken with the voices that others hear instructing them to murder their Children or cause any other harm, hurt, or hate on someone else. They claim the words come from God, or that God is showing up in the form of that person, but that is all inaccurate. The voices of God, Heaven, and Spirit will never instruct someone to hate, harm, or hurt themselves or anyone else. Those are the voices of that person's ego. The voices coming from God are always empowering, uplifting, and full of love even when warning of danger. These are traits that are the opposite of an individual claiming to be of God. Heaven instructs or offers messages and guidance that can help that individual or another person positively and with compassion. Those who are clairaudient will hear things that no one else can hear.

Claircognizance

Claircognizance means "Clear Knowing" (or Clear Knowledge). Someone with claircognizance will receive messages and guidance from Heaven being dropped into their mind. They will typically announce something that they have no way of knowing only to find that it comes true. When asked how they know this information, they will be unable to efficiently answer that question. They have no idea how they came to receive this sudden insight. The messages sifted into them out of nowhere. Someone will say, "You're absolutely right! How did you know that?" You'll look at them stunned and say, "I don't know. It just came to me."

Those who have strong claircognizance are the thinkers of the world who bring positive change such as inventors, scientists, teachers, speakers, research investigators, and writers. These people are usually skeptical about where the information is coming from. They might not believe in God or an afterlife. They need concrete evidence before they become a believer, but even then they still function with some measure of uncertainty at times always looking for concrete tangible proof. When someone exhibits claircognizance, they have the presence of someone in control and in command. They always seem to have the answer for anything and everything that ends up assisting others in a positive way. Their mind is constantly 'on' and in motion making mental lists that periodically come to them all day long throughout each day. When you receive a lightning bolt of an idea out of the blue that brings you success, then you can be assured that your claircognizant channel is functioning in top form.

Perhaps you're driving through a new town with a friend only to discover that you're both lost. You ask for heavenly assistance and then blurt out, "Turn left up ahead." When you turn left, you both find that you're no longer lost and know where you are. This is an example of receiving assistance through your claircognizant channel. On another scale, someone with deep claircognizance would be someone like Alexander Graham Bell's connection with the invention of the telephone or Thomas Edison and electricity. Claircognizance is "knowing" the answer to something. You know what's coming up ahead or how something works. The information sifts into your consciousness from seemingly out of nowhere. This later proves true or is positively helpful to you or someone else.

Someone with claircognizance has a tendency to tune everyone out unless it's a super important bullet point. They're the ones that interrupt others while in a conversation to bring their expertise or examples to what the person is talking about. They cannot help it as the information, guidance, and messages flows so effortlessly through the individual's claircognizance channel. This isn't to be confused with someone who interrupts others repeatedly for the sake of attention and to hear themselves talk, although many claircognizant people may do that. The messages the claircognizant picks up on come through with an underlying tone of excitement. Suddenly the messenger cannot control themselves and need to share it immediately.

Someone with claircognizance may have difficulty sleeping as the thoughts in their mind never shut off. This isn't someone who has the occasional restless sleep over an issue that's happening to them personally, nor is it the restless sleep conjured up by a stressful time in your life. Claircognizant people are always tossing and turning from birth until human death, even when life is going great. Some of them may be prone to taking a sleeping pill, herbal relaxer, and even something harder at night. Otherwise their mind will never shut off and they'll never sleep.

Claircognizant people are always thinking and others tend to comment that they can see their wheels always churning. The claircognizant loves words and communication, whether that is being an avid writer, passionate reader, enthusiastic speaker, or all of the above. While musicians and singers are more apt to having clairaudience, someone with claircognizance would be the songwriter of lyrics. The clairaudient would be the one jotting down the musical notes since they hear the sounds. Because claircognizant people tend to have the right answers or know what to tell others that can assist that individual, this makes them the go to person whenever someone is having any kind of issue. It is rare for the claircognizant to go to anyone for advice, since they already 'know' the answers naturally. If they do go to someone else it's to compare the wisdom or get another point of view since they are a lifelong teacher/student.

Those who incarnate from the Realm of the Wise One have a strong claircognizant channel and tend to make excellent counselors, inventors, problem solvers, and writers. It is not uncommon for someone who has incarnated from the Realm of the Wise One on the other side to be a non-believer of anything beyond the human physical life. This is because they desire scientific or concrete evidence. Wise Ones operate primarily through claircognizance where the answers to questions they're not versed in seem to fall into their consciousness naturally. Like the claircognizant, a Wise One will rarely go to someone else for answers, wisdom, messages, or assistance, because the Wise One is the chap who is approached for that knowledge.

Clairalience and Clairgustance

Clairalience means "Clear Smelling". Someone with clairalience smells scents that are not happening in real time or on this plane. You might suddenly smell Cedarwood and recall that this was the smell that your Grandmother used to have in her house. Yet, it's coming out of nowhere in the place where you live. This sudden scent around you that is not physically explainable can be that you're picking up on the presence of your Grandmother.

Clairgustance means "Clear Tasting". This is when you taste anything that is seeping in from the spirit world. You can be lying in bed and suddenly you smell a foreign scent or taste chocolate and yet there is no rational place for the scent or taste to be coming from. You haven't eaten anything resembling chocolate and there are no smells burning anywhere near where you live that could resemble Cedarwood. This is a basic example of how to tell if you have clairalience or clairgustance.

How can I tell what is me and what is my Guide or Angel?

When it's you talking then you will hear the word, "I". It will be bathed in either dark ego or negativity such as, "I'm not qualified to write about this topic."

When it's your Guide or Angel, then you will hear the word, "You". It will be immersed in love or optimism. This voice will say something like, "You will write about this topic as you are qualified more than you realize." The voices of spirit are of a high vibration and filled with uplifting love that assists you or someone else in a positive way. The chatter in your mind causes confusion and chaos pushing you to act on those voices. Anything urging you to hurt yourself or someone else in any fashion is the chatter in your mind and not God. Voices from spirit are direct, optimistic, and filled with compassion and love, even if it's sending you a warning. The feeling of being trapped at times is another sign of one having high psychic abilities. You're more in tune than those who operate from pure ego. The trapped feeling is also the absorbing of the harsh energies being darted around this planet. You're absorbing it without intending to.

Run tests such as keeping a journal or notebook and record the information, messages, and guidance that you think is your Spirit team. Revert back to the notebook over time to see if what you wrote down ended up coming true or had a positive effect. If it did, then you know it was heavenly guidance. If it didn't, then that can also help in deciphering that it was your ego or an estimated guess. With continued practice, you begin to notice when the guidance you pick up on is more on the mark or not.

Working With Your Spirit team

Your Spirit team is the lineup of players in your
life that reside on the other side in Heaven working
with you and guiding you along your Earthly life path.
They are made up of one Spirit Guide and one
Guardian Angel. They are present with you when you
are born into a life in the Earth plane. From that point
on your journey, they remain with you until you meet
up with them again when you pass on from this
lifetime. If you are someone who works with Heaven,
angels, guides, or any other benevolent beings, then
you may have more than one guide and angel who
come to your side. Some may stay permanently with
you, while others will come in specifically during
important junctures in your life and then leave once

you have accomplished what needs to be done. The way that one's teammates on a Football team in America have each other's backs because they are considered family, this is the same way your Spirit team has your back and vice versa. You work together with them.

Let's say that you are spending your days longing for a romantic partner. If your Spirit Guide and Guardian Angel are working with you on other day-to-day situations, then you may have another guide or angel who joins you in your life assisting you on your search for the kind of soul mate that would be beneficial for you. This Spirit will work with your soul mates Spirit team in order to bring you two together.

You could be a busy professional and not active in the dating world aside from joining dating sites and dating apps to get to know potential suitors. Or perhaps you have done that and it resulted in disappointment. This assigned "love guide" works with this other potential's guides to help you two to connect. You find you suddenly start crossing paths with the same person repeatedly at the store, at the gym, in an elevator, or even in a parking garage. There is a reason behind running into this same person consistently out of the blue. You are attracted to them, and you notice they seem to be taking notice of you in a positive warm way, yet you both brush it off or do not act on it. This is partly due to your ego and partly how technology has trained others to communicate via technical devices, but rendered them incapable when face-to-face. Both of your Spirit team's will continue to work on getting you both together. Yet it is up to the both of you to do the rest of the work. This work includes something that might be difficult for some such as saying, "Hello."

If you find that every time you run into this person, the butterflies rise, you grow nervous, or feel inadequate, then mentally in prayer ask God and your Spirit team to help give you confidence and courage. What's the worst that is going to happen if you make a mistake by saying, "Hello"? The other person says nothing or reacts in a way that wasn't what you were expecting.

It is difficult for two people coming together in this day and age where primary means of communicating to each other is through technological devices. Now you're standing in front of someone and you're suddenly a mute. This other person is likely just as nervous as you. They might be kicking themselves for not responding adequately. If you continue to run into this person, you'll both grow more comfortable with the other one being around. It will get easier to begin conversation even if it's always a, "Hi, how are you?"

There are no missed opportunities. If the soul mate you are intended to connect with is meant to happen, then it will.

There is something called the "Free Will Universal Law". This is God's law, which says that all souls have free will choice. God, Heaven, and any spirit being are not allowed to interfere or intervene with your free will choice, unless your free will choice is going to result in death before your time. And even in those instances, your Spirit team is not always able to prevent premature death.

Some have asked how God can allow misfortunes happen to people. If you're on the freeway speeding and not paying attention to your Guide and Angel nudging you to slow down and pay attention, then there is only so much they can do to prevent an accident. This fate results in your death and others deaths based solely on your free will choice to act out in a way that is dangerous and detrimental.

A pilot of an airplane took down a plane and crashed it into a mountain with 144 passengers on it. When someone is at the helms of a manmade vessel with 144 lives in that one person's hands, then those passengers on the plane are under the rule of that one person. You might say those passengers did not deserve to die. Perhaps they prayed and no help was forthcoming. An aircraft is soaring in the Earth's atmosphere with someone who is operating on free will. They ignore any heavenly guidance that is dropped into their consciousness. Their Spirit team is doing whatever they possibly can to alter someone's state of mind. Those that chose to board the aircraft might have done so on free will choice. Perhaps they made a prior agreement that this is how they would complete their Earthly life run. Perhaps their own team was nudging them to not get on the plane. By the time they realized something wasn't right, it was too late to pray and ask for help. As stated, no heavenly spirit being can interfere on any human soul's free will choice, without an expressed invitation via mentally, out loud, or in prayer. This is God's law.

Interesting to note the strong angel numbers 144 connected to how many passengers were on the plane. Coincidence or is it?

More people than not are saturated into the physical material world. They have been trained by each other on how to function, behave, think, and what to go after in life. They are technologically based, which has its plusses, but the flip side is it blocks one from paying attention to any guidance being filtered into them from above. There have been cases where an accident has taken place, and someone who survived recalled feeling (clairsentience) something foreboding beforehand.

When a catastrophe or accident happens, it is intended to wake others up to implement strategies that can prevent such a disaster from happening again.

How often do you sense something is about to happen and it does? Or you hear a voice inside you stating something that later comes true? You have free will choice to choose which path you would like to take, but choose wisely. Heading down the wrong path will result in a dead end or cause something catastrophic. The damaging effects of free will choice are showcased all around the world and in the media. Some countries feed their children unhealthy diets, because it's all they know or it's all they can afford. Children are raised on these diets, and when they grow up they raise their Children this way and so forth. This is the same with someone's values and beliefs. They gain that knowledge by how they were raised. It doesn't mean they're right, because it's all they know. The evolving or advanced souls are the ones that break away from that mold and realize there is something bigger than what they've been trained to know. They are aware they have a purpose here.

You ask Heaven and your Spirit team for help and you receive. You ask people for help, and you may not receive. Others have protested to ask God for help, but nothing has come to fruition. They stop believing and their faith dwindles. If what you're asking for can only happen with the help of someone else, then you cannot blame Heaven when it doesn't happen.

The Power of Prayer

The power that comes with prayer is out of this world. I've been testing the power of prayer with phenomenal results. Ask God and your Spirit team for guidance in prayer, through an affirmation, or in writing. The traditional ways others have prayed are with your hands clasped together, or kneeling down in a Church or by your bed. The truth is that it doesn't matter how you pray since God knows what's in your heart. You can say one thing, while attempting to shield another. What is hidden is what God and your Spirit team already know. This is why you cannot get away with a lie in Heaven the way you can with others on Earth. An Earthly soul who has strong a Claircognizance channel knows when someone is lying.

You can sit against a tree in a quiet park with your thoughts and those are prayers too! You are always communicating with God whether you're aware of it or not. I made it through the difficulties in my life with the power of prayer. There are those who protest they do not believe in praying. They make fun of others and harass those who do it and tell them that they're speaking to nothing in the sky. This could not be further from the truth. I have always had a scientific analytical skeptical mind and I've been communicating with my team since I was a child. I've been testing them for decades! When I say testing, this means that I would report on when I've prayed and what I've asked for has come to fruition. When I've not prayed, then I would notice that nothing has happened. I wouldn't continue with something if there were no results. The power of prayer is real and alive!

It's understandable that some are skeptical about prayer, but mostly it's because they're anti-religious due to the media portraying only the worst of the people who are religious and the hatred and crimes they've committed in the name of a false God called their ego. The media ignores the good religious people who love and accept all regardless of that person's interests or lifestyle choices. Praying has nothing to do with religion. Anyone can pray from an atheist to a spiritual person and you are being heard. Sometimes non-believers are praying without realizing it. They've admitted to sitting quietly with their thoughts at night with the things they desire or want to see happen. Through that act, they are praying. Praying is connected to the law of attraction which is connected to positive thoughts bringing in that which you desire.

You ask for help in a prayer and it doesn't come to be. You immediately believe Heaven is ignoring you or God doesn't exist. He exists within you and all living souls. The power of prayer is out of this world. I know that because I've been praying since I arrived here. I've asked for help and I've eventually seen my prayers come to fruition. Sometimes it was immediately and other times it was gradually over time.

You help some of those prayers along by taking action where necessary. This is also by paying attention to your Spirit team in order to follow any instructions given.

The second you demand something in prayer it will not always be granted like a wish to a genie in a bottle. There are life lessons you must endure before gifts are bestowed. There are reasons for the delay. Sometimes they are waiting for you to wrap up a toxic relationship and bring it to a close before they offer you the big career position you desire. Or they are waiting for you to make that move you've been thinking about to the new city where what you want is waiting for you.

The angels will never put you in a situation that will end up having a negative impact on you. You make choices that sometimes seem as if you were reading the signs correctly only to later discover you made an error in judgment. The more you work with them, the easier it gets in deciphering what is indeed your Spirit team and what is not. While it's important to keep ones heart open to others, you also need to be on guard to an extent so as not to be taken advantage of.

With the angels it's about letting go of the control and allowing what is intended to fall into your lap naturally. If you feel the slightest bit of doubt, or a tinge of an uncomfortable feeling within, then that would be a sign to back away from something. The angels can be super subtle, which is why they push for you to be clear minded and to watch what you ingest as your senses are highly calibrated at that moment. When your senses are calibrated, then so is the communication with them.

Your guides will give you information that will come out as if it is a future prediction, and then it doesn't come true. You'll begin to believe it was your imagination. If you went to a psychic reader, and a prediction did not come to pass, then you would believe they were wrong and denounce all professional psychics. Psychic readers are not God, and neither is your Spirit team. They have no control over what someone does or doesn't do. They only see the projected outcome. This outcome changes from one day to the next pending on anyone's free will. While there are some psychics who are interested in taking advantage of a client, this is not the case with every single one. Just like any group, there are both good and bad involved. The best psychics are only about 75% accurate on a good day. Even though they, like you, were born 100% psychic, the heavy Earth plane with all of its toxins and blocks dims that considerably. It blows right back up to 100% when you cross over back home to Heaven.

There is a job you truly want and so you ask your Spirit team for assistance in obtaining that job. If your Spirit team knows that this job is aligned with love and your higher self, then they will get to work in helping you attain this job. How they might do this is by connecting you with the person at this job who would be responsible in hiring you. If you're paying attention to the guidance of your Spirit team, then you will discover who the appropriate person is to contact at this job. You meet your Spirit team half way by getting your resume together and forwarding it to this employer.

Your Spirit team then contacts your employers Spirit team behind the scenes. This is in order for them to begin nudging this employer in getting that person to notice you. They may keep dropping clues in front of the employer such as getting your resume to the top of the stack. If this employer is not paying attention to the nudges and guidance that their Spirit team is putting in front of them about you, then it becomes challenging. As a result, you start to believe that your Spirit team is ignoring you and not helping you get the job. You have to keep an open mind and understand that this is not always the case.

There are several factors that come into play as to why the job offer is not happening. One of them being that this employer is not paying attention to the messages and guidance being put in front of them about you. There are a great deal of human souls who are now disconnected to anything outside of them, including the assistance of their own Guides and Angels. They do not have to believe in Heaven to notice the messages. Employers have pointed out that someone's name was constantly being put in front of them. They did not understand why, but went with it and called that person anyway to offer them a job.

Your Spirit team is wrestling with someone else's free will, which people use quite bit of! Many do not listen to or pay attention to the nudges of their angels. Don't just ask for help, but believe that it is forthcoming and already here. If you feel abandoned by God and your Spirit team, then ask them to boost your faith. Those in Heaven would never desert the soul they're assigned to look after and guide. The reverse is that many people abandon God and head down the path guided by their ego.

It's also important to know that Heaven cannot fix everything that comes at you. You are placed in situations that you put yourself in based on past decisions. Your team will keep you away from eminent danger that could result in extreme harm or death before your time when you work with them, but they cannot ensure that everything is in working order and tip-top shape. You can drive your car all over creation everyday and hope that nothing ever happens to it, but eventually something will. It will need to be serviced, the tires will need to be rotated and changed. Some of the work is up to you to take the bull by the horns and take action on.

You have a crush on someone and want to run into them again. You ask for help and continuously run into this crush every so often. You both stare at each other with interest, but say nothing. You grow depressed thinking maybe that the crush isn't interested. You ask for help again. Your Spirit team can get you both in the room together, but they cannot make you talk. That's up to the both of you to do. It's like someone can get you a job interview, but it's up to you to get the job. You're a self-sufficient thinking human being. You're not a puppet on strings that Heaven is controlling or making you walk and talk.

How do they get you and your love interest in the room together? They do this by communicating to the both of you through your senses. If you're both paying attention to your senses, then the quicker you'll have your answer on whether or not this is a go. Your team works with the object of your interests Spirit team to place the claircognizant idea into your mind. When this happens, then you suddenly say something like, "I need to go to the store today. I think my crush will be there." And sure enough your crush is there! This is also why it's important to work on raising your vibration and watching what you ingest, since a raised vibration equals clearer communication with your Spirit team. You're able to pick up on the messages and guidance filtering into you from your team such as when to go to the store to bump into your crush.

Mark, a reader of mine in his twenties, moved into an apartment where a neighbor's cigarette smoke was blowing in the wind and into his place. He was furious and didn't want to close his windows since he enjoys fresh cool air breeze blowing in, but not mixed with nicotine smoke. He asked and prayed for some kind of resolve. He said, "I like this person, but I can't do the cigarette smoke."

Gradually over the course of several months he noticed the cigarette smell was gone. Eventually the neighbor ran into Mark and informed him that he quit smoking recently. He added that he was suddenly being nudged to quit. Over time the prayer helped as Mark saw the results.

When a catastrophic situation happens in your life, the immediate emotional response is panic and anxiety. While in that state, it lowers your vibration and cuts off the communication from Heaven. Not to mention you forget to ask for help while in that state of mind.

Jennifer, another reader of mine, has been in those situations where a circumstance like this has happened and she's moved into panic mode. She immediately asks for help in an alarmed state. She realizes, "Okay I need to calm down and trust that help is forthcoming. Quiet my panicked mind knowing how devastating this situation is at the moment. Ssshhh. Close my eyes. Ask for help calmly."

Within the hour of the prayer, the situation is miraculously resolved and all is well again. She admits to feeling foolish afterwards for having panicked in the first place.

Humanitarians have quite a number of Guides and Angels that have entered their life to work with them. When the humanitarian has those frequent moments of wanting to throw in the towel or they doubt God, then that persons Spirit team lifts their heart and mind in order to motivate the soul to continue on. Sometimes they do this by infusing a sudden burst of energy that is an uplifting motivating feeling within you. This is after hearing your prayer or cry out for help. For some, you agreed to an Earthly life for a specific purpose geared toward the world at large. When you falter on your path, your Spirit team coaxes you onward.

I go into detail on psychic reading related guidance, ignoring heavenly messages, as well as karma and Heaven's gate in my pocket book, *Spirit Guides and Angels*.

The Earthly Birth

Heaven, the Spirit World, and the Other Side are all the same place depending on whom you talk to and how that soul prefers to label it. You are a soul in a human body living an Earthly life for a purpose. Some souls have many intentions, while others have one big objective. There are also universal goals, which include learning to love or bringing others together in a positive way. If you were born to love and that comes innately, then you are a teacher of love. You lead by example in expressing that love full time naturally.

My Spirit team has shown me through clairvoyance on numerous occasions over the course of my life that in Heaven there is no darkness or pain. It is a paradise filled with immense light and flickers of magical sparks of color. This light covers anything that can be filled. This means it is in every soul, cell, plant, desert, mountain, ocean, human or animal on all planes and dimensions that exist. You may call this light God, a Higher Power, the Source, Spirit, Light, or any other name that is comfortable to you. In Heaven, this light has no name as it just IS. The names and labels are what human souls use in order to differentiate, describe, or single out something that needs no separation. We use it here so that the soul can have a quick understanding of what we are talking about. The light affects all that it touches with the same positive results. It brings on a sensation of overflowing love, peace, and joy.

This light consumes you in a magnificent way that brings an out of this world uplifting sensation as if you're going to fall over or burst apart. It's an exhilarating high that cannot be obtained by any human made drug, food, or drink on Earth. If you've ever been in love with someone who loves you back, then you understand the rush of excitement and joy that is experienced when you both touch one another let alone sit in one another's presence. This is because love releases your soul from the confinement it suffers through while having an Earthly life. This same rush of excitement from a lover's touch is magnified one hundred times on the other side merely by being in Heaven's atmosphere.

When your soul steps into this light, then any negative feeling you're experiencing is blasted away immediately. When a soul crosses over to the other side and enters this light, then all emotional, physical, or mental deterioration that soul was battling with on Earth diminishes. If you had what is considered to be a handicap, then this is removed and exists no longer as your soul travels back home. The handicap is a temporary condition connected to the physical body vessel you're using temporarily in one lifetime, but it is not the true state of your soul.

This is why you want to avoid singling yourself out with labels such as having a disease or handicap that you identify, with unless it's relevant to a cause you're fighting for. "Hi, I'm Mary and bound to a wheelchair because...." Or, "Hi, I'm Bob and I'm HIV Positive." It may be a physical human disease or handicap that has attacked your physical body, but it is not who your soul is in truth. It is a temporary human physical disease or handicap that goes away when you leave your physical body. Who you are is Mary or Bob, a loving and compassionate soul who gives to others generously through your empathetic activism.

If you own a car, you do not say, "Hi I'm so and so, I drive a BMW and I work for a law firm." You are not the car you drive or the job you work at. Yet these are the physical, material, external things that people focus on. When one meets someone new, they immediately go down the generic list of human taught questions such as, "What do you do for a living? Where do you live? Where are you from?" None of those things matter in the long run. They are just something you are affiliated with today at this point in your life, but your job and car do not define you. Who your soul is at its core is who you are and what defines you.

My Spirit team has explained that your soul sometimes chooses a handicap in order to develop a different perspective, or for a specific purpose or goal that the soul must discover on its own. The challenges of this handicap contribute to soul enhancing and growth properties that the soul might otherwise not gain if they were not having that experience. To my ego mind, I could express doubt, but to my higher self's space and what my team relays, I receive it with an open mind and disburse the information publicly by allowing others to decide for themselves what they're comfortable accepting to be of truth.

"Doubting" partially comes from the ego part of a soul not wanting to believe something is possible or for real. Doubts are concerns and worries where you require additional concrete visible answers that will bring your ego to a higher level of comfort and peace. It adds security to ease the skeptical part of you that is questioning, because your higher self has no doubts. Doubts can also signify a warning nudge from your Spirit team preventing you from heading into danger. When you cross over back home your soul and physical self is restored to top form appearing around 25-34 years old. Even though some souls may temporarily appear to be the age they passed away at in order for them to be recognizable to you.

On Earth, someone might have a cup of coffee to wake up in the morning, or they might have a glass of wine or a beer to wind down after a long day at work. Sometimes they do this to let loose and have some fun since the life they currently live feels joyless and restricting. There is little to no love experienced in one's life. When you're high in love, you rarely yearn for a drink or drug. This light in Heaven is your cup of coffee or bottle of beer. You do not crave a vice back home in Heaven. The state you attempt to achieve while living an Earthly life through vices is reached naturally on the other side.

Your soul light is born out of what some call God. God is not a man with a beard sitting up on a throne looking down at everyone waiting to cross you off His list. Nor does He desire to throw you into a brimstone and fire like setting if you've made mistakes. God is a force that is within every soul light including the faithless and non-believers. How unconditional of Him to still love someone who makes mistakes. His love for you is bountiful and endless. He is the light that over takes every cell that exists in all dimensions and in all paths. When you feel and display traits aligned with love, joy and peace, then the closer you are to God. The more negative traits you experience or display, then the further away from God you are, and the less light that occupies your space. If someone is persecuting or bullying others in God's name, then you can be assured they are nowhere near God or the Light. The exception is if it is done to prevent someone from harming or hurting themselves, or someone else.

Heaven advises that you exhibit assertive compassion in those instances, rather than aggressive bulldozing. The latter comes from uncontrollable emotions from your ego that take flight beyond that soul's control. There is a healthy ego and a dangerous nasty ego. The horrible ego, or darkness of ego, is never at peace and thrives in the shadows by multiplying and growing. The dark side of the ego is a murdering terrorist, while the light side of the ego is someone who displays confidence over what they can accomplish and do in their life. Someone who is sure of themselves has a healthy ego, while someone slamming or criticizing someone who is confident and sure of themselves, is operating from the darkness of ego.

There are newborn souls and there are advanced souls on Earth in a human body. Newborn souls are the student souls who immediately enter into an Earthly life upon being born out of the Light. It is generally their first life run on Earth. Advanced souls have been around the block so to speak. They are the teachers, inventors, leaders as well as movers and shakers. Newborn souls tend to be on the naïve side and use the most amount of malicious ego. Naïve might be too innocent of a word to the damage this soul causes, but in the eyes of the angels "naïve" is the word they give me.

The newborn souls are easy to spot as they instigate the most disruption and donate the largest amounts of negative energy while contributing harmful pollutants that cause tragically damaging results on humankind. They might be the soul who spends their days criticizing others in an unhelpful way by posting malicious comments at everyone or those around them. They name call, bully, and put others down. The targets they hit can be over someone's physical appearance, or if that person does things differently than they do, or lives in a way they do not approve of, then they will attempt to assert domination over them. In the end, they are unsuccessful since the light ultimately overpowers the darkness in the end.

Those people who exude that energy full time are someone you do not want to be around or spend that much time with if you can help it. They will lower your vibration and cause enormous quantities of inner or outer turmoil. They will create roadblocks that prevent you from moving forward and lead you down the wrong path often without trying to. You might be stuck living or working with someone like that. You want to steer clear of this individual, as they are what the Devil is.

Not all baby souls wreak havoc on others in a negative way. There are just as many good newborn souls as there are bad. The newborn souls who are good tend to be the ones who evolve and advance their souls growth at a rapid rate. A newborn soul can also be someone who is without drive to accelerate or improve themselves and their soul. This is because they do not have the tools to do so or do not know any better. Their soul's energy is rendered stagnant in those environments. They might be governed by their ego and doing what they were taught to do by their families, peers, and society around them. They are a product of their surroundings going through the motions of how they were trained to by others during their human developmental years. They elect to come back and have another Earthly life in order to polish up and advance their soul. Some of the newborn souls are destined for greatness, but are growing up in a setting that does not support soul growth, but rather restricts it.

If you're aware that you're not like everyone else and you feel like the outcast in your surroundings, then this is a sign that you are a gifted soul waiting for the right moment to make its mark on humanity, if even to allow your soul's light to shine as brightly as the Sun on those around you. The road will eventually lead you to that place naturally on its own time.

Where a newborn soul might follow others, an advanced soul would be the leader who takes charge and goes against the crowd. They manage to rally up equal interest and opposition in the process. Advanced souls know without a doubt they are here for a purpose. They also understand what that objective is. There is no question or doubt about it. They might struggle in young age, but eventually will dive into their purpose at some point in their life. An advanced soul is a disciplined individual. It is someone who is contributing something positive towards humanity, themselves, or others in some way. The advanced soul elected to come here at this time.

The Soul and the Spirit

The soul and spirit labels are interchangeable. You are a soul in a human body. You are also a spirit in a human body. Your soul and spirit are one in the same. The terminology has grown confusing since the definitions attempting to describe both have become vague. This is because they are compatible. When you describe who you are beyond your physical body vessel, then using either the soul or spirit name is acceptable. It has the same meaning to describe your consciousness and the real you when you strip away all physical attributes. It is the soul part of you that takes physical form and inhabits this body you function in. Your spirit consciousness is a thinking feeling soul. Your soul and spirit are your life force.

Someone might say after the ending of an unhappy relationship, "This connection broke my spirit." It is a metaphor because your spirit can never be broken. What they mean is that it broke their heart. Not their physical heart, but their heart chakra's life force. It lowered their vibration and gave them a temporary crushing emotional feeling that made them depressed, hurt, and distrustful of others. These feelings are a natural reaction after a heart broken relationship experience.

When you are born into an Earthly life, you're flowing with abundantly high vibration energy that cannot be contained. This energy is your life force. As your soul moves into a human physical body, it becomes contained and suppressed to a good degree. The soul often feels suffocated dying to get out. It will seek out ways to achieve this including in unhealthy ways. High vibration energy is located in the space your soul lives in before you enter a human physical body. This energy resides within your soul's core. It is always accessible even when you feel disconnected from it, or when it's been severely lowered while travelling along your Earthly life journey. An impenetrable wall might surround it, but it is still in you deep down for access. You can either try to work on bringing that energy force out, or wait until your physical human death when it bursts out of the body you inhabit and you're brought to your soul's natural state. It is wise to bring it back to its most instinctive state possible, rather than live a life in permanent misery.

This high vibration energy is shattered over time at the hands of the society that surrounds the newborn human child. This is made up of your caregivers, your peers, your community, society, the town you live in, and the media you engage in. They naively impose their often-harmful views that create an array of seemingly impossible roadblocks and hurdles for that child of God to climb out of. For some, it may be that you were born into an abusive household, or at the hands of a caregiver who viciously inflicts values in you that cause you to despise others because of their life choices or who are different from you. Hatred for an entire group is taught to you by your community, caregivers, and peers. This includes hating or disliking anyone who is of any race, religion, sexual orientation, political affiliation, gender, and so on. You lump them together in one group to express your disapproval of all. This is not coming from a place of Godly love. You may know someone like this, or you might even admit to yourself when you've been guilty of separating others out of anger. Your higher self will correct it when you realize you've crossed the line and are not viewing things clearly. There are bad people in every group, just as much as there are good.

The ego views circumstances in a perpetual hazy darkness. You have discovered the hate filled ways of the darkness of ego simply by logging onto the Internet to see how humanity behaves. Technology is a great invention to bring others together much more rapidly than before, but it also shines a light on how humanity truly is at that given moment in time. When there was no Internet connection or media, then people went along with living the way they were trained to by those around them in that particular area. Technology, social media, and the Internet blasted the truth wide open to see that people are not as nice, caring, compassionate, and loving as one might have thought they would be. If every single human soul accepted what everyone is choosing to do without judgment, then there would be less anger and discrimination. This is highly unlikely to happen while human souls remain governed by the darkness of their ego. It is also not realistic because when a murdering terrorist is physically harming one of God's Children, it's difficult not to be revved up to do something about it.

You are fighting in the name of the Light to protect all souls that cause harm on another. Causing harm on another soul is a sin. Many human souls need to be trained how to behave, which is why so many Warrior of Light's and souls from the various realms continue to choose to incarnate on Earth throughout history. This is to contribute something positive that brings Light to the planet while also improving human behavior and its existence and way of life.

Your peers might be those who continue to tell you that something is wrong with you because you're different from everybody else. The ego has a difficult time accepting and loving those who are unlike it. The ego finds that person weird, unusual, and uncommon, while the higher self sees every soul as one. If you've been the recipient of that abuse, then it might have made you feel like an outcast, inadequate, or incompetent. You spend your life trying to prove that you're not different in order to fit in. Or you avoid going after anything you want to do as you feel you won't be good enough and will therefore be rejected. Avoid allowing others to influence you into believing any of that. That is the soul's dark ego, which views circumstances and its surroundings in a limited way. They are at a place in their life where they are unable to access the broader view that Heaven sees.

When one raises their consciousness, the spiritual portal begins to open up and the Light pours into you. This Light shines brightly and brings the real truth out. This truth is one that the dark ego has a difficult time absorbing and would prefer to keep hidden. The positive extreme reaction by those who are treated as an outcast is that you accept that you are different for a reason. You have a greater purpose and mission, and nothing will stop you from accomplishing that. You are proud and confident that you are not like the others.

If you have been called a derogatory word such as weird, unusual, no good, or any other belittling words, then this is one of the many clues that you will receive in your life that you are indeed destined for greatness. It is the unusual ones who have a higher quotient of being special than any other human soul. They are the ones who are more connected than they realize. You are being beat up on by others, but do not allow the human ego in others to push you down. You have great power and stamina within to rise above them knowing how awesome you are! Who you are at your core is a perfect soul child of God and the Light.

Pay no mind to the naysayers and negative critics around you and access this source from within to be the best that you can be. When you have God in your house, then everything around you becomes irrelevant and trivial. Imagine what it feels like to know there is no element or trace of darkness within the Light. Visualize this Light filling you up with pure joy, peace, and love. You step into this Light and it immediately blasts away all traces of negative feeling or thought. This Light overtakes your physical body, your spirit, soul, and mind.

Have you ever had a love crush on someone? You know this crushing love feeling inside you runs deep and intense to the degree that you never forget it throughout your life. Perhaps you were with someone who reciprocated this love, but then one day they took it away. You try to understand how someone's profound loving feelings for a soul could shift to complete bored disconnect. To not value that soul with enough respect bemused you, but in the end it made you that much stronger. Multiply that love crushing feeling when it felt incredible while in the throes of love. Even while multiplied one hundred times, the feeling doesn't come close to what it's like while being immersed and part of the Light.

A "spirit" is also a name that human souls gave those who they perceive to be entities. These entities reside in a different plane than the Earth dimension. Some have used the word, "Ghost", while others think of spirits or ghosts to be translucent or opaque. This is how they might appear for someone who is clairvoyant, but in reality they have physical bodies. It is not the same physical body that a human body is. They appear in any shape or form they desire to morph into. The physical body they display cannot be harmed. It is in its perfect state and can shift from male to female if it pleases, or into a light source or other figure.

Hell is on Earth and Satan is the darkness of ego in human souls. God, the Light, and Heaven see your true nature and who your soul is. Who it is at its base is all love, peace, serenity, compassion, and joy. These are some of the highest vibration qualities that are aligned with God and bathed in Heaven.

A murderer's soul is seen with love. This doesn't mean they get a free pass. Somewhere along their Earthly life, the dark part of their ego took over and chose to do anything in its power to sabotage that soul's purpose. Their ego could have been developed and programmed as early as age three in human years. When the soul exits the physical body and crosses over back home, then it is faced with choices to make that can bring the soul to redemption. Some of that entails another Earthly life in a less than stellar circumstance than their current one was. Other souls are put to work and take the long way around through the back gate of Heaven.

There are some dark love undertones to this. Perhaps your lover's soul gets lost in limbo or ends up in another realm and you never see them again. In reality, it's not impossible to visit them should that be the case, but from the human mind's perspective, the worst is generally feared. When you cross over, you move onto other destinies that are not always the same as someone else's, including your loved one on Earth. Still it is possible to travel and visit one another once you've crossed over. This travelling to see them happens in a matter of seconds.

Your soul is the spirit part of you that is not part of your physical human body. Your human body is a temporary vessel your soul is renting out for a limited time. When you're born into a physical human body, you enter this life through a human female. This is the beginning of one lifetime for you. This human body starts out as a physical human infant and grows up and ages over the course of a short amount of time. In Heaven, it is the opposite where ones basic appearance remains the same. On Earth, the human body is limited and for some those restrictions vary in endless ways.

Some choose to enter this life in a wheelchair, or you might have asthma issues, or another human physical limitation. When you are connected to spirit, the boundaries are non-existent. You are loved beyond measure in Heaven. It doesn't matter what or whom you've chosen to live this lifetime as. Whether you are male or female, rich or poor, gay or straight, religious or atheist, and no matter what race, or political affiliation you choose, all are seen through the eyes of Heaven as being equal. The separate labels are what the ego mind chooses in order to feel superior or separated from others, when in truth all labels are irrelevant. Using labels creates separation by viewing reality in a limited way. When you only see the love in someone else, then you're able to access the parts of that person that the angels see.

The angels see who the soul truly is when stripped of its dark ego. When you become defensive or argumentative every time someone says something, or you get upset over every news headline, then this is coming from a place of ego and your lower self. There is no truth or love while in that space. Seeing the love in others is seeing life through their eyes and having an understanding of what their reality is like. This does not mean that you're accepting someone's bad behavior or horrible words they might have darted your way. If that's the case, then it's best to cut them out and extricate them from your vicinity. This is about taking issue with the small stuff in a profound way that it does nothing to help anyone.

Some hang onto anger over trivial issues such as a friend having to cancel a lunch date on you since something else came up that they needed to do. It's giving someone another chance and offering forgiveness to anyone who desires to make amends with you. If someone is interested in strengthening your connection because they feel horrible about the way they behaved, then hear them out. Too often others have a wall of anger, "She has some nerve calling me to say she's sorry now."

Holding onto anger breeds a mold like Cancer within your body that spreads and slowly attacks you. When you come from a place of love and acceptance, then the cold parts of the emotions you're feeling evaporates. This doesn't mean you have to be best friends with someone again, but hearing them out and thanking them with compassion is taking the high road. It is being diplomatic and civil with no traces of animosity in your heart. You no longer have to engage with them if you choose not to. Leaving it on a high note is operating from your higher self.

I have a cold temper and hold slights close to heart over those who exhibit poor etiquette, but this is also the mark of someone incarnated from the realm of the Wise One and their distant cousins, the Elementals. It's their job to correct others in the name of the Light, so I understand the difficulties that arise when you're trying to see the love in someone else who has done wrong in your eyes. You realize the naivety or selfishness that someone else has shown and it can get under your skin.

These angelic rules are guidelines that contain a structure much like the Ten Commandments had the intention of doing at that particular time in history. It's to train human souls to grow, expand, be compassionate, become better people, stronger, and more evolved. In the end, none of the stresses, anger, and negativity that you experience has any bearing on anything once you've passed on and travelled back home. Suddenly whatever you were holding a grudge about will be trivial and irrelevant. Call on your Spirit team to help you in the areas where you're having trouble forgiving someone for something erroneous. This benefits your well-being as well as everyone around you. Release toxic emotions to Heaven for transmutation.

The way you learn to see the love in others is by seeing the love in yourself. See your soul in a way that God and the angels see you. To them you are perfect in every way, even when you fall down and make mistakes. When you plummet down a path of addictions, they still love you and want you to accept and love yourself. There is no judgment despite what some might believe. There is no discrimination because they view you in a broader and more profound way that is difficult for a human ego to comprehend.

Your Guardian Angel is the one that lifts the pain off your heart that drives you to an addiction to cover up pain and to forget about life for awhile. Someone who operates from a lower vibration will have distaste or be repelled by someone who is confident and self-assured. This is considered a threat to the dark part of one's ego. Someone who is evolving and looking to build, enhance, and grow their soul is attracted to someone who exudes confidence. They admire someone who loves and appreciates themselves as well as other people. Pay no mind to those who attack or bully you for being sure of yourself. You are operating from a higher frequency by standing in your power and loving the totality of you. Love all that you are and shout it out from the rooftops, and from the highest mountain, because you are magnificent.

The Significance of Spirituality

Spirituality is asking the bigger questions and being open to the understanding that there is much more to an Earthly life than the physical material world of narcissism created by human ego. Someone can consider themselves spiritual if they are religious and go to Church regularly. They can also be someone who enjoys going to New Age stores, playing with Tarot cards, or reading self-help books. The spiritual person can be someone who is solely interested in improving ones well being and subsequently the way they live and their quality of life. The list is long as to how deep the Spirituality genre can go and what that individual identifies it to be for them.

Someone who considers themselves to be a spiritual person will more than likely be curious, interested, or at least open to all facets of the genre. This is one who is interested in deeper philosophical knowledge as to why they are here or how everything was created. They want to know how to improve themselves and this world. Their belief in God will vary from believing in some form of higher power to not believing in any type of God, Light, or spirit. They might follow and enjoy all facets of spirituality, but will not believe there is any kind of God. God also has different meanings for people depending on who you talk to.

A spiritual person who does not believe in any kind of God is not to be confused with an atheist who tends to not believe in anything, except that when you die you're done and all goes black, the end. An atheist does not believe in God, an afterlife, or any form of metaphysics, spirituality, new age, religion, or God. Even though they might lump the entire spiritual genre together, generally they take issue with organized religion, God, the Bible, and religious dogma. They find the mere mention of an afterlife to be hogwash, and any hint of spirituality to be New Age phooey. An agnostic is someone who is more open minded to the possibility of some form of God or afterlife, but they do not fully believe in it, yet they also do not fully believe that there is nothing after this either. They hang in the middle requiring physical evidence to convince them. They're more likely to be open to spiritual pursuits in order to assist them on their quest for this knowledge.

I've witnessed atheists transitioning into having more of an open mind when they get their toes wet in any level of spirituality that they feel some form of comfort with. They receive a big enough jolt in their life that leads them to begin "questioning" and thus becoming more of a spiritual person or agnostic. There are atheists who might not believe in any of it, but are still drawn to spiritual or self-improvement books and interests. In a sense, they're not realizing at that moment they're moving from atheist into an agnostic. All human souls are spiritual beings regardless if they believe in that or not.

Earth and all of the planets came from somewhere. They did not suddenly appear in a perfectly orchestrated solar system that affects the energies in humankind depending on its planetary path. An explosion did not create a set up of planets that circle the Sun in a flawlessly designed fashion and then permanently stay that way. Pluto is the only planet farthest from the Sun to be detected by humankind. This does not mean there are no other planets or galaxies beyond that, as there most definitely are. Humankind is just unable to detect that. No other life form outside of Earth has been detected scientifically after eons of centuries gone by. As big as the universe is, all life forms seemingly only inhabit Earth, or so one believes.

Seven billion people on Earth in this solar system at this time in Earth's history are not an accident. This also gives you some perspective as to how miniscule humankind is in the grand scheme of things. You venture off into space to planet Jupiter or Neptune, then suddenly life on Earth appears immensely ridiculous and trivial from that distance. All of the fighting, disagreeing, pollution, harm, and negative words darted back and forth to one another make humankind look rather silly. You can get a pretty good idea as to how Heaven views the planet from where they are. All of the nonsense that goes on means nothing to them. They watch everyone hate, hurt, and harm one another and roll their eyes with indifference so to speak.

Others find it difficult to believe that God, the archangels, and the angels are unaffected by the harm people are doing to one another. This is thinking from the ego and in a limited way. God, the archangels, and the angels are egoless, which means they have no ego. When you have no ego, then you're unaffected by anything. It does not mean that you do not care, but you are not ruffled emotionally. An egoless being witnesses harmful destruction and feels nothing. You have a detached perception. You view things from a higher perspective. This is not to be confused with a murdering terrorist or serial killer who is without a conscious. They have a dark ego that governs their life demanding they kill. They want control, which is an ego trait.

When you're upset, then this is your ego. God, the archangels, and angels do not get upset because they are egoless. Someone might say operating from ego, "God will punish you for that." This is that person's projection of hoping that God will punish that person, but God does not chastise.

There are ego beings in Heaven, but their ego is not out of control the way it would be in the Earth's atmosphere living a human life. Go back through centuries of history to the beginning of Earth's conception and the start of humankind. At least one man and one woman would have needed to be present in order to multiply. It is not by chance that they were suddenly here and figured out how to mate. They did not evolve out of apes and then stopped evolving out of them. They did not rise from the dirt and appear. There are circumstances existing that are larger than the human mind can comprehend. Science has attempted to make sense of it all, but without much luck since the initial creation of life, the planets, people, animals, plants came together in ways that a non-believer wouldn't be able to fathom or comprehend. There is no data that exists of when the first man walked the Earth and what that was like. There was no language or concept of anything being what already is. The spiritual connections were stronger at the dawn of humankind because there were limited distractions and blocks that ego would later create within them.

It was human instinct to connect sexually and suddenly people were being born and multiplying at a rapid rate out of that. They soon believed that it was God's purpose for them to continuously procreate. Breeding intelligently is one thing, but multiplying to seven billion people shows that most reproduce out of ignorance, naivety, and to fulfill ego desires. Earth is a rapid ant farm with people screaming and starving for attention, power, and domination.

Every living soul is a descendant of the first man that walked the Earth. No one is separated by color, culture, or any other factor. The darkness of human ego caused separation from one another. When someone is not evolving, then they view their surroundings and other souls in a limited way. They are uncomfortable with anyone who is different from them being in their vicinity. The ego will grow angry and cause them harm, hurt, or hate just because the other person is not an identical clone. The ego sees this person as threatening, instead of viewing others with understanding, love, acceptance, and compassion.

You move into the realm of Spirituality when you start asking the bigger questions such as, "Why am I here?", and "Why are some people different?", or "Is Heaven Real?" You understand there is much more to life than the mundane physical existence that has been structured and set up by human beings of years past. As a spiritual person you have a belief in a higher power, energy, light, or life force. You have a belief that when your life run is complete, that it is not the end. Someone who is spiritual has their own personal barometer on how things should be. They might not necessarily believe in God. The teachings within the spiritual and religious genre tend to differ while other times you'll find there are some common parallels aligned with one another. The similarities are give and take by varying degrees.

One who is interested in spirituality is open to expanding their consciousness and seeking out the solutions unanswered for them. It is an individual quest to align your soul with energy bigger than the material plane. This is working on your soul and becoming a better person in the process. You want to be connected to what's beyond the current life you're living.

Sometimes one is not born spiritual, but as they evolve over the course of their life they grow to become spiritual. They might have hit rock bottom, which prompts a major transition that awakens that soul and raises their consciousness. They could have been raised in a strict religious upbringing that felt wrong to them if it was enforcing shame, guilt, and other negative feelings that are not aligned with God. To their subconscious, this feels dishonest as they recall their connections while in Heaven and where they came from. They do not remember it to be a place of hate and assault. Suddenly, they find themselves hip to this reality. Why do people commit horrible deeds? Why are others cruel to one another? These are some of the questions that one desires answers to that can make some measure of sense to that soul. If God exists, then how can He allow bad things to happen?

I have deep connections and communications with spirit beings that consist of guides, angels, saints, and archangels. This is no different than what anyone else can do when they elevate their consciousness, raise their vibration, and tune in to what's beyond. While it is true, some people are more strongly connected than others in general. All souls have the capacity to elevate their consciousness, vibration, and clair channels to be equally connected. Every soul connects to the other side whether you believe you are in communication with your Spirit team or not. Sometimes you think that the accurate information you're coming to is your imagination or you second-guess it. Examine all of the varying belief systems that humans have designed and invented. From that point you connect the dots to where the truths within each belief system reside. There are some common denominators and similarities such as all paths lead to God. What others feel God to be is up for individual debate. The higher evolved human souls sense that in the end that it's all supposed to be about love. The further you stray from love, the more disconnected you are from spirit and God.

There are teachings that instruct you to not crave material wealth as that is a detachment from God, and that the only way to true happiness is from within. While this has some measure of truth, many shun this belief just as much as they reject strict religious doctrine that insists you will go to Hell for something like French kissing. These dogmas need to be corrected and illustrated in a way that is easily digestible. The detachment from materialism needs to have the right balance, because the way Earthly life is designed today is by prospering the economy. This is the current Earthly life reality whether you agree with it or not.

Human beings need to make money to survive, to eat, to be clothed, and obtain housing. People designed it this way over the centuries of history. They implemented new ways of finding work through the rise of supply and demand. In the process, they grew detached to anything outside of themselves. You get up every morning to drive to a job to make money to be able to pay your rent or your mortgage. Most people spend the majority of their waking hours at work. This is more than at home with family, friends, and loved ones. You're taught to meet someone, get married, move in together, and start a family. These are the basics, which sound easy enough, but in the current modern day world it's grown much more complicated than that. People have a difficult time finding a partner in crime to be with for life in a love relationship. And when they do finally find that person, it doesn't always last until the end of their days together on Earth the way it used to.

Humankind is taught how to function and the mass majority moves along with that trend. They're taught to go to school, graduate with a High School Diploma, and start thinking of College, or look for a job. They're taught to hate others who are not like them, and pass judgment, or cause harm against those who live life differently. You can be spiritually connected and still thrive to find great work that fulfills you in order to make enough to live comfortably on this planet. There are differences between becoming obsessively money hungry that you are viewed as an angry miser, to being someone who works hard, and does their job well, but you're not ruled by this job.

When you remember who you are, and you have a stronger connection of what is beyond, then the answers become clearer, and God comes rushing in. Your consciousness is its own thinking, feeling, and soul inhabiting a human physical body. You are bumping into other souls inhabiting a body as well. They are also their own thinking and feeling soul inhabiting a human physical body. Why are you here? What does your consciousness remember? Your consciousness is the part of your soul that continues to grow wherever it moves along its life path. Your soul has been to many places. One child recalls repeated dreams of seeing both a red planet and a black one. Another child vividly remembers Christ making him.

In essence, when any soul is born they are spiritual at heart. They are 100% in tune and psychic. They are full of immense love, joy, and peace. The soul knows where it came from. As the child grows, its environment trains them to be who it prefers it to be. At that point, you stray further from the spiritual genre. Yet you're having an individual spiritual journey. If you're an atheist, then that is your current spiritual journey. This is the same if you're Buddhist, Christian, Catholic, Muslim, Agnostic, and so on.

The kind of spirituality we promote is where you get to be yourself as long as it's not hurting you or anyone else. You get to be as raw, crass, and different as you like. In some spiritual circles others have mentioned that they feel judged by someone who is on a different journey than they are. Slamming others, harassing them, and name-calling is not being spiritual, or a good person for that matter. This is different than the ego resorting to reacting out of anger because someone has attacked them. We're talking about those who go out of their way to criticize someone for not doing something the way they might do it. This is not someone operating from their higher self. Everyone is on a different spiritual journey including a non-believer. That is their journey they've chosen to go down. As long as no one is hurting anyone, then allow that soul the freedom to explore what works for them.

Warrior of Light

There are souls living a human life that are threaded around the planet called, "Warrior of Light's." A *Warrior of Light* is a soul who fights in the name of Heaven, God, and the light. They are often the darker souls who ferociously defend and teach in the name of the light. Typically unwavering and unbending, they are representatives of the Light, but have no problem rising to head into battle, which they're called upon to do often. Archangel Michael is the General of all Warrior of Light's. The Light is God and God is the Light. They are interchangeable energy and the all knowing source. A warrior of light is someone who is a fighter or soldier for God and Heaven.

Imagine a company created by Heaven called, "The God Organization". You are one of the employees. When you need supplies, you ask God for these supplies. Sometimes He might temporarily deny the supplies due to budgetary constraints, but He is a fair boss and will provide what He believes is best for you at that time.

The Warrior of Light is not a role I'm playing, but rather it is a part of me. I do my job when I can as if I'm working for anybody else. I have *off* days as any human being does. The difference here is that I love this employer. When you like your employer, then it's not a drag to do the work.

The Higher Self

Earthly life is tough for millions of souls. It feels like an uphill battle that never ceases. To put your soul under so much pressure that it ultimately crushes you is the kind of heaviness that Heaven wants to prevent you from experiencing. For some, it results in premature death due to the compounded stresses you've placed upon your back. Life does not have to be that hard. When you come to the realization of where this resistance is coming from, only then can you begin the process of experiencing true freedom. This freedom is what your soul craves. It longs to be released from the confined ridiculous structure that human ego has designed. Avoid falling down the path of destructive addictions or suicide to get away from the chokehold this life has on your soul.

Earthly life today has a never ending supply of material distractions such as cell phones, computers, jobs, rents, mortgages, poor diets, toxic relationship connections, lack of exercise, stress, depression, and the list goes on and on. All of these things and much more block the divinity within reach. This holiness is accessible and resides within your innate nature. You do not need to search for it or move to another area to find it. You're carrying the answers within you.

People live in big cities on top of one another and that contributes to the suffocation of your soul. This is why implementing soul enhancing practices when possible can assist in lightening this load and make living in nearly any condition somewhat better than manageable. When you walk through an empty park or garden, suddenly you begin to feel calmer and more relaxed than you were before you went out into nature. Your mind awakens and clarity seeps in with an attempt to yank your true higher self's nature out to dominate again. There are basic ways to reach that serenity space where you're reminded that God is with you. Many avenues in which your soul can find this freedom exist. Hatred and negativity is a poison that chokes you. Putting in an effort to display love, compassion, and fun will lift you up allowing your soul the freedom to float above the clouds. This soaring feeling is where you grow closer to God. You have pieces of Him within you, therefore you are Him. No soul is exempt from this despite what they may or may not believe.

You are perfection through the eyes of all in Heaven. The "you" that is the truest you is your Higher Self. Your higher self resides in a more sophisticated state of awareness. It can be obtained by rising above any negative thoughts, moods, or toxic consumptions. You reach that higher space when you are clear minded and centered. You have access to this higher self since it is the true you. The false "you" is the one that struggles against the current.

Put your higher self back in charge whenever you find you've been faltering into negativity. You can do this by releasing the need to manage circumstances that are beyond your control. You accept and detach from that which bothers you. Work on letting it go since it is not worth it in the larger picture. You do not need it. Invite Heaven into your life to guide and assist you in this process. You can do so by sending out a request to God and your Spirit team mentally, out loud, or in writing.

Bringing yourself to your natural state is where you see things through the eyes of love. Your higher self requires nothing because everything is as it should be. If a mistake is made, your higher self learns from it with indifferent emotion and moves on. Your higher self efficiently corrects the mistake without drama, because it knows that all is well. This is just an Earthly life run and should not have to be so complicated. It becomes complex when you are mired down heavily in physical desires and functions. You have to get a job and go to work to make money to survive. It's understood that this is how physical Earthly life is. You can still go after the physical necessities you require without getting obsessively bogged down in it that it stresses you out or makes you permanently unhappy.

To move into your higher self's state is to not desire to "want". What you want may not be aligned with your higher self's state. You may want someone specific in your life in a love relationship, but this person is not someone that will be on an equal footing as you. Heaven sees someone else on its way into your life that is aligned and around the same level as you spiritually. This is why most souls attract in those who are similar to them to a degree. When there are vast differences in vibration to someone else, then the connection grows challenging and sometimes breaks apart. Exceptions are balanced Teacher-Student relationships where there is a compassionate give and take.

Your vibration is moving up and down throughout each day depending on what is being thrown at you. This is why it can be difficult at times to be in your true self's state around the clock on this turbulent planet. Your day starts out fantastic and you are in your higher self's state. You are happy and full of love. You get in your car and someone cuts you off, or honks their horn. You suddenly feel stress and agitation. This gradually moves you into your lower self's state. That is until you bring yourself back up to that space of feeling centered and at peace again.

It becomes a juggling act or a yo-yo as you learn how to adjust your frequencies throughout any given day. You might say, "This would be easier if I didn't have to deal with people." But this is not necessarily true. You could spend all day at home alone and not doing much. Soon you reach moments where you feel unmotivated, lonely, isolated, secluded, or bored. Those states gradually begin to lower your vibration into your lower self's state. No one caused it, but the negative thoughts in your mind. This is one of the challenges of living an Earthly life.

A pioneer conquers new territory by being themselves and going against what the masses believe in order to promote positive change. Think for yourself even if you stand alone. Stick to your guns even if others disagree or attempt to bully or attack you. It is more than likely that you will be bullied and attacked at some point in your life if you haven't already. The dark ego is threatened by those who are strong, different, seemingly rebellious, out spoken, or a know it all. Pay no mind and stay focused on your life purpose and goals. Someone may confront you at some point in your life. Lower vibration human souls are threaded out among those who operate on a higher level. The lower evolved is threatened by someone who rules at life. Ignore that kind of energy as it's irrelevant. You have a job to do, so refuse to back down or fill yourself up with fear that you will not be popular by going against what is expected of you.

For some, the idea of an afterlife is considered to be a fairy tale that gives one hope for those who fear death. This is false and a belief that is conjured up by those who do not experience day-to-day connections with source. They might have never reached that one defining moment in their life that convinces them enough that there is more beyond their physical existence. The more in tune you are, the more you are likely to have profound experiences with the other side that perk up your ears.

It is difficult now more than ever in history for a human soul to connect with something beyond. They are distracted by the physical demands of Earth from buildings, cars, phones, computers, electronics, drama, violence, negativity, and noise. The list of blocks between humankind and Heaven are endless. This has led souls to grow up on Earth not believing in anything spiritual related. To believe that there is a God that sits on a throne above the clouds casting judgment and waiting to punish man is the real fairytale, but God is another name for all that is. Every cell, every atom, and organism that exists is God. He is everywhere filling up all available space possible in every plane, realm, universe, and dimension. You cannot run from Him.

There are some who do not believe in an afterlife. They have come to this conclusion due to a strict religious upbringing that was filled with negativity and judgment. Or they might not believe in Heaven because life has dealt them a poor hand. They might end up being confined to a wheelchair and they look at that as a negative. Often those situations are a result of accelerated spiritual growth needed. When one finds that at some point in their life that a major handicap or challenge has taken place, it's intended that you begin to view the world and all that is around you in a broader or different way. The goal is to awaken your mind if it was previously closed. The other case is the handicap came upon someone because the physical body is not infallible. It will be met with challenges that evaporate when you head back home to Heaven.

An atheist will protest to not believe there is another place one goes to when they pass on. They believe that when you die it's the end. Although some profess to be atheists, they are more agnostic when they reveal statements aligned with the belief that your mind is open enough to allow room for the possibility of there being some form of God or afterlife. This is pending they are able to receive concrete material based evidence on that, otherwise the conclusion is that it must not be true since they've never seen it. The evidence will not show up in a math equation. The data exists when you fine tune all of your senses. You open them up a crack to receive a divinely guided message convincing enough to the ego that ultimately helps you ask the bigger questions and notice the possibilities of more being out there.

I have been testing my Spirit team and Heaven out my entire life. I do not blindly follow or believe in something I cannot see. I have an analytical mind and require some measure of proof that convinces me, so I understand skepticism. I've had repeated occurrences where I've stated something that was about to happen and it later has. Everyone has that connection and at one time or another may be able to recall those instances where they've noticed this same phenomenon.

The ego cuts off the communication between the non-believer and what exists outside of them. Your ego is what sabotages you and tells you that you're not qualified and have no business doing anything you want to do. Your ego's voice instills fear and causes your life to feel chaotic, while the higher self's voice is filled with overflowing love, calm, or excitement. Your ego's voice changes its mind daily and often, while your higher self's voice is stable, faithful, and frequent. Your higher self's voice will continue to push you to do the same thing repeatedly for years until you finally do it. That voice would never urge you to do something that would ultimately bring you or someone else down. There is a domino effect to your decision making process. When this happens, it is clue that your choices were made from the ego.

Your ego pushes you to take action in ways that cause pain, hurt, or confusion, while your higher self's voice gives you brilliant flashes of ideas that never leave your mind. When you implement them into action, you experience success, love, and joy. The ego will make you feel as if you're bouncing around, stagnant, heading nowhere fast, or going around in circles and never accomplishing anything. While your higher self pushes you to make changes that benefit you and others. It might coax you for decades to finally write that book! While your ego will delay you from moving forward and will say you're not qualified to write a book. It'll tell you that you don't have the time, or it will instruct you to wait until you're more settled. When you listen to that voice, you can be assured that you will never accomplish anything and nor will you ever write that book.

You hear those who are of older age express regret, "I should've done this or that. It was always on my mind too, but I never did it." Right there is a clue to the heavenly guidance you were receiving most of your life, but you ignored it. Those listening to their higher self's voice are suddenly filled with glorious love and excitement. Pay attention to what's going on inside you in order to decipher what is your higher self and what is your lower self. Examine the repercussions, challenges, or blessings that come out of that as a result of your action or inaction.

Life Purpose and Soul Contract

Your life purpose is what gives you joy. It is what you would do for free if you had all the time and money in the world. Your life purpose is your passion that assists and benefits you as well as others. If ones purpose is to live a life showering the world with love, then this is an objective that brings both you and another something positive. God and your Spirit team know what your life purpose is. They know what plans have been mapped out for you, but you also have this knowledge embedded deep in your subconscious too. It was something you agreed to before you chose to live an Earthly life. You can discover the answer to what that is when you tune in within. Your life purpose is not a question that can be answered by anyone, but yourself.

Every soul has a *soul contract* drawn up before they enter an Earthly life. Within this contract are the terms of your life purpose, as well as some of the key Soul Mates you would encounter while living an Earthly life. These experiences with the various Soul Mates met along your path are intended to contribute towards positively enhancing your soul and to bring you to the next step on your soul's journey. Your Guide and Angel work with you in your life to ensure that you stay on path. This is why it's also important to be in tune and pay attention to your Guide and Angel. Staying on path is to help you fulfill the terms in your contract. When you're in tune and connected, it's not difficult to know what your purpose and terms are.

Sometimes you might be privy to what the terms are as circumstances happen for you. You might experience heartbreak in a love relationship and then say, "Now I know not to get involved with someone who is married and has no plans to leave their spouse." You gained major soul and life enhancing skills in the process of the experience. It strengthened you to be on the lookout over who is a quality mate and who would not be good for you. These situations that happen can be something that is in your soul contract. If it isn't, then it is the result of your free will choice, since no being in Heaven can intervene on your free will without your permission. Free will can at times cause an array of delays along your path, not to mention poor life choices. When you're not connected and in tune, but are guided by your ego and lower self, then you find that its one roadblock after another. You spend your entire life running around in circles chasing your tail. You do not realize what's happening until many years in. You discover, "Wow, what have I done the last five years?"

When your terms have been completed, you may exit this lifetime at that point, but not always.

Sometimes one might fulfill their contract, but then will spend the remainder of their life working in a career that is their life purpose. They become of service to others, or choose to spend their days enjoying their retirement since they've fulfilled the terms in their contract. They've spent their life working hard on their life purpose and they deserve a break of luxury and relaxation. Sometimes finally having that break is when they find their life purpose if it hadn't been discovered in ones earlier years. Luxury and relaxation are two qualities that Heaven wants to see all souls experience on a regular basis. They see relaxing and taking time outs as a necessity for your soul in order to recharge. These acts are near non-existent today thanks to the break your back work all day everyday set up designed by the soulless. The soulful understand the benefits to working hard and smart, while also taking regular time outs. When you take regular time outs, breaks, days off, then you are more productive at work. You are stronger, healthier, and have a better attitude. This concept has yet to seep into the consciousness of many in the work force.

Not everyone's life purpose is ones chosen career. Many life purposes are not geared towards monetary success. Monetary success does not contribute to soul enhancing qualities, unless the millionaire is a humanitarian who uses their money to assist those in need. This charity is an important character trait in enhancing ones soul.

Not everyone fulfills their contract and in fact a great many number of souls do not complete it. This is one of the many long lists of reasons as to why some souls opt to come back for another Earthly life in order to fulfill the terms of the contract. Saying this to someone having an Earthly life now would prompt them to say, "Oh no, I'm not coming back here." The ego says that because the person's current life experience or the state of the world today is not satisfying to them. However, on the other side, you have a much broader perspective. You're in a different space with far less ego. The soul wants to come back in order to fulfill its purpose or to assist the planet in a way that no other is doing.

Journalist, Oprah Winfrey, is a humanitarian that used her money to help others in a positive way. One of them was by opening up the, "Oprah Winfrey Leadership Academy for Girls in South Africa". She's contributed millions of dollars over the years to help those suffering from poverty as well as towards others in making their dreams come true. She had an inner drive to do something positive with her life. She went after her dreams and achieved it. She then took the gift of monetary success and used it to help others in a positive way, which ultimately became her true soul's life purpose. This gave her and others joy.

This is one example of how to determine what someone's life purpose is. Your life purpose can be as big as being a friend to others the way Jesus is to the underdog. Some of his followers of today ironically turn against or criticize the underdog.

Not all life purposes can turn into a full time career. For some it is a side hobby that you enjoy doing. Brian, a twenty-six year old man, set up a website to help people. This enables others to email him for advice. He has made himself an open door for others to discuss their problems with him. He doesn't charge anyone, but also doesn't care about that. He is fulfilled knowing he's been able to help at least one person. This is his life purpose. He discovered that it brings him and others joy by being of service.

It's important to understand that the world we live in requires that you must make money in order to survive. It's not like it was centuries ago when you could barter your services, which is giving someone something of value for something of value in return such as food and housing, etc. Over time human beings moved away from that and demanded that you use paper money for things. This gave money power over people. The ego in human souls will at times do whatever it can to obtain what they want. They will push others down to climb to the top of the ladder or they will steal merchandise they want in a store.

Greed has overpowered the human condition, which is also why bartering wouldn't survive today. You cannot trust humankind to be honest. There is nothing wrong with charging for your services as this is the way Earthly life is set up now. You cannot pay your rent with sticks and stones. You have to get a job to make money to pay for the necessities of life such as housing, transportation, clothes, and food.

In Brian's case, he has a day job, which is his primary source of income. If he deeply wanted to pursue his passion and life purpose full time, then he could begin requesting some measure of payment for his services. Never quit your day job to pursue your life purpose hobby, unless it is safe enough to do so. This means your life purpose brings in enough income for you to survive so that you may safely leave your regular job. This is a dream that many would love to have. Not everyone wants to work in the rigid, cold, corporate environments. The way that Earthly life is set up now is that it's not as challenging to create your own business that is aligned with your purpose. Most everything is online now and you can create businesses and services online without having to lease out a building to set up office. That's a major expense you're saving. There are some businesses that would require you to lease a space. An Esthetician wouldn't be able to work on someone's face unless the client is in the room with them. The Esthetician desires this kind of work. They are attracted to beauty and physical appearance upkeep. This is their life purpose because it brings joy to others through health, beauty, and self-care.

No one can tell you what your life purpose is. This is something that you must come to realize on your own. How can someone tell you what your purpose is? Only you know what brings you and others joy. This is for you to decide, not someone else. My life purpose is writing books and entertaining or teaching through the written word. Not only does it bring me joy fulfillment, but I learned to understand that this has also been helping people around the world. To receive a note from someone in Turkey, Japan, or Australia who loved one of my books and had to tell me is pretty cool.

Not all life purposes are intended to bring in an income, so there is no need to worry that you've found a life purpose that isn't bringing in money. The key to knowing if it is your life purpose is if it brings you and/or someone else joy and assistance. You would do the work for free if you had all the time and money in the world. It's something you find yourself doing because you want to.

When you have free time from your day job, you are excited to dive into your life purpose fun. Your life purpose doesn't feel like work to you. It's something you enjoy doing. Life purposes can also be helping the masses in some way such as working in a homeless shelter or traveling the world to assist those in need of basic life saving supplies. It can be painting on a canvas and showcasing your work in a gallery. Art brings others enjoyment, therefore it is that artists life purpose. A concert performer enjoys putting on a show and the audience benefits by having a good time. It takes them away from their mundane lives. This performing action is the band or singers life purpose. You will know it is your life purpose when you find that this is an activity you would participate in when you're not at your day job. It doesn't feel like work to you.

Darkness of Ego

The angels are egoless and only see the love that exists in each soul no matter how buried deep that love is. When you have no ego, then you crave nothing. You are unaffected by anything related to darkness or negativity. You operate from a place of innocence, which is not to be confused with naivety. This virtue is a super high vibration energy that is filled with love, joy, and peace. There is no room for any low vibration energy since it burns up before it hits the aura of the angel. God, the Archangels, and Angels are the only beings that are egoless. All other souls have an ego, which includes human souls, departed loved ones, most realm souls, ascended masters, and saints.

When one exits the Earth dimension and travels back home to Heaven, the dark part of your ego is reduced to a spec, but it is never fully diminished. If a soul crossing over avoids moving into the light, then the dark parts of their human ego continue to operate in high form. This is no space for your soul to be stuck in.

Mediums have uttered words from a departed loved one with that soul's ego intact. This might be seen when your Grandmother is relaying a message to the Medium that she thinks that the person you're dating is wrong for you. An egoless being would never say someone is wrong for you. They would only impart the challenges that can arise with the one you're currently dating. They would relay the words from an objective space leaving the free will decision on what you choose to decide as being up to you. Whereas, someone coming from the place of ego would say, "I don't like that person for you. I never did."

The departed soul has not gone through training where one of the traits learned is detachment. This means you allow all souls free will choice without interference. The exception where an egoless being would tell you what to do in that circumstance is if the person you are asking about is abusive in any form. The egoless being or trained spirit guide would lovingly direct you away from that person. Guides are called 'guides' because they're guiding you, rather than making you do something. They'll point in the direction that is best, but they won't make you head down there. That decision is up to you. You are the manager of your life.

The angels also see the innocence in the actions of one who is not evolving. They see who that soul is in truth and not what that person's ego has allowed them to become. They know the soul has the capacity to evolve since it is designed in a way that allows one to expand or decrease their light. This does not mean that an egoless being condones the violent acts on Earth perpetuated by dark human souls.

This is to give you a frame of reference as to how precise their insight is. It's a surveillance camera which hones in like a telescope into one's heart and soul revealing who they are when they were born into an Earthly life. Somewhere along that soul's journey in the human body they lost their way and became influenced and attracted to the darkness. This is done through naivety, since someone who is aware already knows the common sense differences between right and wrong.

As a soul gets knocked around to get a little street smart, Heaven's intention is that the soul learns the lessons from these experiences. If they do not, then the soul lives a life filled with bad luck, negativity, or even violence. When the soul learns a lesson, its light expands a little each time. It gradually dissolves fragments of the darkness of their ego to a good degree. The dark part of your ego is always there, but you can reduce its domination so that your higher self is what rules your life. You grow and become more aware and in tune to reality, which is not the physical material world reality, or what your peers and surroundings have taught you. You begin thinking for yourself since you are your own moral compass when it comes to what is right and what is not.

The media is one of the largest offenders of emitting negative toxins into the air. They use sound bites and pick up stories from one another to talk about. Often times what they're relaying is not of truth or fact, let alone objective. They influence the mass majority of human souls. It is rare that the news reports on positive stories, and even when they do the readers will still find something negative to say about it. This negative energy is a vibration they emit into the atmosphere that affects anyone who happens to read their comments. Imagine what it will be like eons from now.

There are a great many souls evolving rapidly and becoming hip to the idea that something is not right with the media. These souls are the ones that shout, "Too much negativity on the news!" They know how it makes them feel and it isn't good.

A media story shares a positive happy story regarding a celebrity and someone operating from a low vibration comes on to the comment boards to vent out negative words. These comments are lower vibrating energy phrases sent out into the universe.

Someone operating from a higher vibration would say, "I'm happy to hear this celebrity is enjoying themselves."

Although someone who is in the space of a super high vibration will not bother to comment on a gossip story or be influenced much by it to begin with. If you find that you've been sucked into a gossip/media story, then remember to shield yourself so that you don't absorb that negative energy. Those who post negativity are sending it out into the universe, and others are absorbing it into their aura. You read that stuff and suddenly you feel this ugliness sitting upon your shoulders. It brings you down! This is a sign that you have absorbed that energy. You might spend the next hour or the rest of the day in a funky mood because of it. Those who live in that space full time are perpetually ruled by the darkness of their ego every second. That's not a person you'd want to be around if you can help it.

One big social media site was in talks to include a dislike button on posts. By this simple move, they contribute to the rise of the darkness of ego. You don't give Children a toy that applauds them for being egotistical. Venting negativity and distaste over someone else expressing themselves through a dislike button will add to humanity's chaos. It would not be surprising to see others who are anti-negativity begin to use the social media site less. The social media site in question grew hip to that concept not being such a good idea, but it was one that should never have been considered in the first place. Instead they talked about offering smiley emoticon face choices that enable one to express how they feel about a post. These would include symbols for happy, shocked, laughing, anger, sadness, and so on. There is more than enough disapproval in the world. The ego doesn't need access to negative buttons anymore. This exists in plentiful abundance as it is.

There is much ugliness in the world guided by the darkness of ego. You see this in how others treat people and talk to them on any comment board on the World Wide Web. You hear it when someone bullies you or calls you a derogatory name. You witness this in how someone complains in a retail store that they're not getting the discount they want, so they throw a tantrum and disrespect the sales associate. You see this when someone complains that the meal they ordered at a restaurant is not exactly what they wanted. You see this in the horrific violent murders that a terrorist commits on another human being.

From the angel's vantage point, they see who those souls are in truth, even if this makes it difficult for ones ego to believe. Know that just because they see the innocence in these souls who are vicious monsters on Earth, it does not mean they condone or approve of it. What they're illustrating is that yes they see what the darkness of ego creates, and no they do not approve of it, but yes they can still see who that soul is deep inside. At the core of every single Earthly soul is where the space of love, joy, and peace resides. The issue is that the person was led astray and allowed the darkness of their ego to dominate and consume them.

There is no Devil who governs a hot fiery furnace where he tortures sinning souls, but there is a Devil that resides in every human soul. The most loving human soul has a piece of this Devil inside them. Symbolically this Devil is the darkness of ego.

Imagine having the ability or capacity to see the love in the most impossible to love soul. The angels desire that all human souls remember to move into this space of seeing people and circumstances from the place of love. This does not mean you condone or approve of someone causing harm to another, but it's that you refrain from falling into the lynch mob mentality of casting judgment and demanding someone be hanged because they disagree with you. It is not your place to interfere with the results of what does or does not happen to someone. There is a human created structure for a reason. Justice is conquered in this life or when you cross over. No human soul is qualified to decide on the ultimate fate of a soul.

The word sin is not in Heaven's vocabulary, but what is considered a sin is anyone who does any of the three "H's". The three "H's" are: Harm, hurt, hate. You do anything associated with negativity, then that is a sin in Heaven's eyes. There is no judgment where you are burned in Hell and bonfire, as some believe. The judgment you experience is the judging you do on yourself. When you cross over you soon begin the process of what some call a "life review". We're saying, "Life review", since this is a made up phrase by human souls in order to explain what happens. It is not like you cross over and your Spirit team approaches you and says, "Hey, let's start your life review."

Your soul naturally moves into the life review zone. When you cross over, all your Clair channels expand and your psychic abilities increase off the charts. You no longer have the physical blocks that your human life created disabling you from having 100% pure psychic capabilities. In this life review, your clairvoyant channel kicks off by showing you the movie that is your life. It reveals everything you ever did or did not do - both good and bad. Through your clairsentient channel you also feel all of the things you did or did not do to yourself or other people. This is a painful process, which pushes you to begin the judgment. The judging that is going on is the judgment you're inducing on yourself.

When you make amends and forgive any trespasses you have done on yourself or others, then your light expands even more and you move into a Heavenly life. There will be discussions with your Spirit team and Wise Ones on the other side, as well as those conducting the review. What is talked about are whether or not you will have a repeat life on Earth, and if so when. It is up to that soul to choose to do so or not. Because a great deal of your ego is removed, you realize that your class lessons on Earth we're not complete if that is the case. If someone spent their entire Earthly life wreaking havoc, or implementing violence on others, then they will be coming back for a repeat life. This also applies to the three "H"s. Someone who spends their entire life demonstrating hate, harm, or hurt on others will be incarnating into another Earthly life. This next Earthly life experienced will be designed in a way that would be less than the previous life you lived on Earth.

If you were someone with a ton of money on Earth and treated people horribly, then you might come back to Earth struggling to make money that never comes. This is not a form of punishment, but it is way of teaching a student soul on how to grow, expand, and to show compassion with others.

Seeing the love and the innocence in others helps you view human souls from a detached position. The reason this is beneficial is because there are no negative emotions associated from this stance. When you immediately move to anger or sadness over what someone did, then these are negative emotions, which are toxic to your overall well-being. You're pissed off at someone for doing something that is un-cool or against your own moral compass, but your toxic anger doesn't affect that other person. It's you who is affected by it. This kind of energy is what breed's diseases and health issues over time. You're slowly killing yourself when you experience negative feelings over the actions of someone else.

The darkness of ego is damaging beyond comprehension. It inflames, spreads, and expands easily and effortlessly like gas thrown on a fire. There is no way of getting rid of this ego permanently. The angels ask you to view others through their lens. At face value, this is a seemingly outlandish request since it's impossible to get to their level. It is still achievable to do your best in working on allowing the circumstances you cannot control to subside. Do not allow it to permeate your aura. You are the only one who suffers when this happens. You do not need to react in an angry vile comment over a news story that has upset you. Nor do you need to join the lynch mob in shaking your fist with anger over the hottest media story that is all over your social networking page or Internet. This is about picking and choosing your battles. Don't fall into the hole of the hype around you. Avoid going out of your way to post negative words about a political candidate or celebrity you despise. If you loathe something or someone, then ignore it. You certainly do not feed it negative energy. Doing that will bring that which you do not want to you quickly!

A lover has left you abruptly leaving you in shock. Ones natural reaction is that of sadness and depression, followed by anger and revenge. Do not deny the feelings you're experiencing. You are a good person and someone you loved betrayed that. It's understandable to immediately move into a negative space. The evolution of these negative feelings must eventually bring you to a place of forgiveness and understanding. This is where you see this lover from the viewpoint of an angel. You're not saying what they did to you was okay. You're saying, "Yes, this person hurt me and that was wrong of them to handle it the way they did, but through their eyes I can see the confusion they felt while with me. I can't make someone continue to love me. I forgive this person and I release them and wish them well."

You do not have to remain in touch with them, but release the toxic emotions that have buried your soul alive over how they might have made you feel. Purge any negative feelings you have associated towards anything or anyone that causes you guilt, anger, or sadness. This is all lower vibration energy that brings more of the same to you. This is why it is often difficult for some to climb out of this hole once they've fallen in.

Ask your Spirit team for assistance in helping you step aside while they work on bringing your positive life force back. Look past the physical restrictions that have caused you to feel bad or misunderstood, and see that in truth all is well. These are experiences you're learning from and then you move onto brighter circumstances.

Love and Relationships

The relationships you have with others make up a big part of your life. These relationships can positively or negatively affect who you are and the overall state of your well-being. This is why you will want to ensure that you work on raising your vibration in order to invite in higher vibration souls into your vicinity. Avoid or distance yourself from those who are harmful and toxic to you. It can be challenging for someone with a low vibration to connect with a high vibration person, because the high vibration person can sense someone who is not of integrity or who has a low vibration. They will steer clear of someone with a low vibration. High vibration souls are extra sensitive and avoid participating in situations that will wreak havoc on their system. This includes being around toxic people.

When you get close to a high vibration person, you will discover they tend to mostly be friendly, compassionate, loving, and supportive people. The reason we say mostly is because they are ultra sensitive. If someone crosses them, or they sense harsh tampering energy on their souls system, then they may grow frustrated and lash out, or they take off staying far away from the low vibration soul. This is the fight or flight response that those with higher psychic sensitivities have. The way that spirit beings are attracted to the light around any soul, the high vibration human soul is attracted to those with a large light as well.

To those that know a high vibration soul personally, they will say they're good people and not gossips or prone to following the crowd to fit in. They are into improving or taking care of themselves on some level. They are confident and comfortable with being alone and rarely fall into bouts of loneliness. If they ever do, then it comes and goes quickly. It is not part of their basic human nature. When the soul is operating from its higher self, then loneliness doesn't exist in the equation. Loneliness is a trait that comes out of the human condition.

This isn't to say that high vibration people do not drop their vibration or feel lonely from time to time. On average their vibration is dropping and rising all throughout the day. They are aware when it drops, and they begin the immediate work to raise it again naturally. They know what to avoid and what will negatively affect them in order to do this. Whereas someone who functions primarily with a low vibration tends to stay on that level until they have that awakening moment where they realize they need to make healthy life changes.

The human soul who has repetitive negative critical statements to say about someone is operating from a low vibration. A high vibration soul is not the one who congregates around the water cooler to gossip and spew negative words. They're the ones who distance themselves from that. This isn't out of shyness, but because they're not attracted to energy drainers. They don't need it or crave it on any level.

Feelings of loneliness will make you feel empty and miserable while lowering your vibration in the process. It can come upon someone who is bored, feels a low sense of self worth, or craves a higher amount of social stimulation from others. Another person cannot fill these feelings up since this is something that needs to be developed from within you. A high vibration person operates from a higher space and usually does not desire curing someone of their boredom or boosting up someone's self esteem. This doesn't mean the high vibration person does not desire a love relationship. They crave someone who is on their wavelength and of a like mind. They may complain that the suitors they connect with tend to be of a lower vibration. Low vibration suitors might cheat, are non-committal, or emotionally unavailable. They might be someone heavily addicted to a harsh toxin such as drugs or alcohol, and are uninterested in reducing or eliminating it.

High vibration people are catches for someone who wants to go the distance in a love relationship. They attract in others of varying vibration levels including those on a lower vibration. Getting involved with someone with a permanent low vibration is not suitable, as it can affect you and drop your own vibration in the process. It's like a fitness guru who is into nutrition and health, and yet they fall for and get involved romantically with someone who drinks alcohol in large quantities daily. It can be someone who is interested in going to museums and art galleries, and yet they get involved with someone who loves hitting the clubs or bars on a weekly basis. Once they are both deep into the connection, they secretly wonder how they ever got to together to begin with since their life choices are completely different from one another. They might have been compatible from an astrological, soul mate, personality standpoint, yet they partake in opposing activities. This can become frustrating from both sides if neither can accept their differences. It is something that should have been addressed in the early dating stages. Human souls are trained to put on their best face forward when meeting someone. This is a sense of deception, because you can only keep your best face going for so long before your true colors reveal itself to one another.

There would be a running joke in the past with whoever I was dating that I was revealing all the worst aspects of me immediately. This natural method of mine made those potential suitors even more attracted to me. I wasn't hiding anything and allowed it to all hang out on the surface. I joked, "If you can survive this, then we'll get along real well."

This kind of openness rarely pushed them away or turned them off, but instead ended up having the opposite effect. Each of the potential suitors would later say, "You started out by showing me your worst traits, but as I got to know you I realized how amazingly compassionate and loving you are. You mask it with all this other stuff."

I explained I wasn't masking anything, but being my true self by revealing all facets of me up front. This method is the reverse from the norm where you're trained to put on the deceptive face to lure someone into your vicinity. Six months pass and the other person feels deceived as they learn things about you they're not comfortable with. Those who put on a deceptive face up front eventually discover that they have been found out.

I've heard others say that you treat a romantic date as if it is a job interview. This means you show the best parts of you up front. While this is true for a job interview, it's not true for a romantic date. This isn't to say that you behave like a pig as you're getting to know this date, unless being a pig is your natural self. You put on your best face for a job interview, because when you are working at a job you're wearing a different hat. It's a hat that does not include your personal life or who you truly are. A potential romantic partner needs to see and know the real you. The soul mate that is intended for you will love all parts of you, as you will equally with them.

You check certain aspect traits of yourself at the door when you walk into work to focus only the job you've been hired to do. If this interferes with certain belief systems, then it's time to find a job that jives with your morals. You keep your professional and personal life separate at work. You date someone because you're looking to discover if you and the date will be a match for a potential long-term love relationship. If you're hiding important aspects of yourself with this date and you grow deeper with them, soon enough these hidden aspects will come out. When it comes out, your mate will see it as dishonest. For those who have experienced this, they understand that it's a total blow to not have known the person they were seeing was a certain way until far in with them.

Joining into the most perfect romantic duo you will find that issues arise both big or small. What ensures a successful partnership is that both people love and respect each other enough to compromise. The ego does not like cooperation. It only wants what it wants and does not care what you desire. Relationships can go the distance when both people temper their ego and work together as a team communicating effectively. Modern day love relationships are happening during a time of narcissism running high. This has caused love relationships to be massively short lived or not at all.

Everyone and everything is made up of energy. This dictates the kinds of people you will attract into your area depending on the energy you give off. If you're someone who is always negative, then you will bring in those who are the same or who have found themselves stuck with your negativity. They will break away from the connection when they develop the nerve.

The human soul is not intended to endure a solo life, even though most do. This is why there are soul mates you cross paths with over the course of your journey to offer companionship and vice versa. You have more than one soul mate as all souls do. These soul mates come in the semblance of love relationships, friendships, working connections, neighbors, pets, family members, acquaintances, and even people you cross paths with for a day.

You ride up in an elevator with someone who strikes up a conversation with you. They end up saying something to you that has a positive impact. It could be a statement that changes your life. It gets you thinking, or it is an answer to an issue you needed solved. This is someone that was a soul mate in passing.

Soul mates come into your life for the purpose of your soul's growth. This might be done through teaching or offering you life tools that become helpful for you at a later date. A soul mate is the listening ear of someone you feel comfortable enough to talk to about a life issue. They help you through rough times where it would have been more difficult to get through had they not been there.

Soul mates are not all blissfully and unrealistically perfect. In fact, it can be the opposite, since soul mates are human too. They challenge you and prompt you to look at the darker aspects of yourself that you would prefer to keep hidden. The soul mate helps to bring that out in order to help you improve, grow, change, and evolve. They do not bring these things out in an argument or out of cruelty. It is done out of love and with compassion, because they care about you.

Love and relationships are obsolete to the ego. The ego wants control, and this is witnessed in the current state of love relationships. There are more single people than those in serious love relationships for the first time in Earth's history. Many prefer hooking up with someone rather than developing a meaningful connection with them. Technology has killed the long-term love relationship. Before the Internet, social media, and dating phone apps existed, human souls took their connections seriously. They never took them for granted the way most do now. When they would meet someone pre-technology days, they took that person seriously because there was no Internet or phone app to quickly log on and try and meet a replacement. They were grateful for the rare connections they formed. They cared about them and were interested in making it strong and long lasting.

Social media, dating sites, and phone apps are a candy store to the ego. The ego knows that if there is one tiny flaw in someone else that it doesn't like, then it would just log right back onto the app and chat away with more strangers in hopes of finding a replacement or at least a one night stand. Before the rise in technology, human souls did not have that luxury. They took the people they met seriously and developed long term love relationships and friendships for life. Their egos didn't have it that easy to leave everyone on a whim and start chatting around again online or on a phone app. The ego is unable to connect with one person throughout the duration of its Earthly life. It will find excuses to sabotage connections with others, give you reasons to cheat, or prompt you to govern your life from a place of selfishness. On the flipside, someone ruled by their ego fulltime is not someone who is ready to be seriously dating or getting involved with another person on a considerable level anyway.

There is nothing wrong with a human soul who does not desire a love relationship. They may not want one for good reason. Perhaps they're in no position to be in a love relationship. They might not be able to remain faithful to one person, or they are battling addictions. They're uncomfortable with love, emotionally unavailable, or they're not where they want to be in life. You can still find meaningful relationships with others outside of monogamous love connections such as friendships, colleagues, acquaintances, and family members.

When you join another soul in this life, you have formed a partnership and a team. Teamwork involves working together efficiently as if it is a growing and prosperous business. Each soul brings something to the table that the other soul might lack. You and the soul mate are both Teacher and Student where you switch and reverse the roles. When two people have gone into business together and face issues with their company, they don't immediately walk away from it. They sit down together to brainstorm ways of building it and making it stronger. It is interesting that others do this with work, but that it's not considered to do with their relationships.

In the end, the soul longs for companionship or a love relationship on some level. It wants to grow older with someone they feel a strong attraction for. It is the ego that does not desire this. The ego prefers freedom to hook up with random people or not fully commit to anyone at all. Technology and the media have both destroyed the possibility of deep long lasting love relationships. It's not the technological gadget and the media that did that, but it is the individual ego working in the media, or who has access to technology that did. You give an ego power such as a fun and curious toy to play with, and they will break it sooner or later.

I've received cases from those who hook up regularly. After talking with me about it, they admit to doing it for attention and love. In these cases, they expressed that they've been perpetually single and desire companionship, but that it has not surfaced. In the interim, they seek it out through meaningless hook ups. There is no judgment if this is what someone chooses to do. What this is about is the common complaint expressed from someone who hook-ups regularly that they tend to feel even lonelier not long afterwards. Like any addiction or drug, they log back onto the phone app or website to find another hook up to temporarily satisfy their need for love. The suitors they connect with for a hook up mean nothing to them. It's a cycle they struggle with breaking. The others who hook up do so because they want to. They do not want to feel tied down to one person and crave variety. The others who do it are driven by a strong sexual nature to begin with. Technology is cold, aloof, and distant. This is how others are in the dating sphere. There is a detachment in texting and chatting that translates to how relationships function today. Technology has trained the ego to not develop emotional intelligence, nor to dive beneath the surface.

Long-term monogamous love relationships are possible to have despite how it might seem. There are many happy couples that have gone the distance and last until the end. They are loving and compassionate with one another. They communicate regularly and support each other on all levels. Others around see them as a power couple, or a success story, and one to dream and thrive for. In a successful love relationship, it is you and this other person against the world. You understand one another's strengths and weaknesses. You fill in the gaps that help one another grow and prosper. You take care of each other until the end of your days in this lifetime. Everyone is in survival mode and it can feel unusual to the soul to have to endure difficult times alone without any support. This is where you ask God and your Spirit team for intervention during those times of struggle. Your team is loyal and present for you beyond measure.

Avoiding love relationships does not help your soul grow. Necessary tools are gained when you join in any kind of relationship with someone else. After the rise in technology, it became incredibly difficult for human souls to connect with one another in love relationships.

You desire a love companionship, but have found it impossible to obtain leaving you frustrated and dejected. To an extent, there is a certain measure of pickiness. Technology made everyone a star, which expanded the human ego. They have the long lists of what they won't accept in someone else without any room for compromise or movement. If one is that strict over every little thing, then they'll be looking at a life of single-dom. Others refuse to date a quality person who might either be too young, too old, too short, or too tall and so on. While some are looking for some perfect Adonis or Barbie looking person that appears as if they jumped out of a model magazine. These are all ridiculous qualities to have on ones list of what they're looking for. You rule out quality soul mates due to trivial fetish traits and therefore end up single indefinitely. Most of the time people end up with those they would not have necessarily been attracted to. There are cases where someone has a strong attraction for tall brunettes, but in the end they find that the person they ultimately fall deeply in love with for life is a short blonde.

There are common sense qualities that most do not want in a potential long-term love relationship. These are traits such as you don't want to be involved with someone who has a drinking problem, does drugs, is emotionally unavailable, is violent, or has a tendency to cheat and stray. People want someone who is decent, cool, and a loving, supportive friend. They desire someone who is in the connection with them and has the intention of going at it together for life. This is someone you can talk to and open up with. It is someone who loves you and who you love up right back. It is not one person always being the listening ear, but it is a give and take. Even when you do not feel like it, you drop everything to listen to your partner. This is why love relationships are work. You have to put in the work as if it is your job, except you love this job because you love this person.

Some of the highest vibration qualities that exist are activities such as mutual hugging, cuddling, loving, and touching. The soul longs for air to breathe and these actions awaken your soul. Perhaps you had a lover who reached over to hold your hand and you know how amazing your soul felt to be that close to them. It feels as if you're soaring above the clouds and all you feel and know are love. You discover what matters while here and that is love. Love yourself first and you will be that much closer to inviting in someone who is the same.

I go into great detail on the topics of love, dating, and relationships in my pocket book, *Soul Mates and Twin Flames*.

Chapter Eleven

Raising Your Vibration

Raising your vibration is beneficial and essential as it assists you in picking up on heavenly guidance and messages more easily. One of the big things that others want is to communicate with the other side in order to know what their future holds. This is that person's ego running the helms. Even if you are able to connect, this does not mean your future will be relayed to you. Connecting with your team is not for fortune telling purposes. Your Spirit team of Guides and Angels do not live your life for you. What is conveyed to you is on a need to know basis that will enrich and grow your soul.

Every soul is communicating with the other side whether they're aware of it or not. I walk from my car to the elevators in a corporate building and Spirit messages are sifting through me mostly via clairaudience or claircognizance. I'm not doing anything specific to make it happen, and nor am I attempting to conduct a psychic reading. I'm not asking my Spirit team questions as I walk hurriedly to my destination. The messages naturally fall into my vicinity without me wanting it or thinking about it. I was born with one foot in this world and the other in the spirit world. It's been this way for as long as I can remember. This is one of the reasons as to why I'm at times a neurotic all over the place mess picking up on every shred of nuance around me.

Some people connect with their Spirit team as naturally as you brush your teeth. Others struggle to pick up on messages, or they feel they're receiving nothing. Your team never disappears and stops communicating with you. When you feel you are receiving nothing, then there could be a block in your life that you might be unaware of, and your vibration energy has dropped. What lowers your vibration is also a block. It can be any negative feeling experienced. It can be a particular bad food you ingest. Poor diets weigh you down over time. It darkens your aura colors and creates a layer of dirt particles that can only be seen by Heaven or a Clairvoyant. An exaggerated image of this is "Pig-Pen" from the Charlie Brown cartoon moving about with the cloud of dust around him.

When you ingest a diet primarily of toxins, then the toxins become you. This contributes to blocking incoming messages from spirit. When you eat chemically processed foods on a regular basis, then this energy infuses itself into your soul. Think about what kinds of food might have existed at the beginning of humankind and you have a pretty good idea of what is okay to consume. It was over time that humankind began heavily processing foods with unnecessary chemicals, additives, and fats.

Junk food didn't exist at the beginning of time. Eating a healthy diet of fruits and vegetables is what assists greatly in removing blocks. It is also awesome for your health, soul, and physical body. This is not the case for everyone since the way blocks happen are complex for each individual. This is merely a guide of the potential basics that could likely be blocking someone from connecting with Spirit, and thus weighing their energy and life force down.

It's okay to indulge once in awhile. My weakness in my early twenties was Pizza and Beer. As I changed and leaned more towards a healthier diet, my cravings for Pizza and Beer were reduced to next to nothing. Meaning I don't really crave it the way I once did. I'm not opposed to it, but I'm just not thinking about it anymore. Because my tastes changed, so did my palette. You train your palette to become used to what you're eating whether it's good or bad for you. If something tastes weird that's good for you, it won't be long before you become accustomed to the taste and it doesn't bother you so much. It wasn't much of a fight when I began juicing Cucumbers in my twenties. It is like drinking water and I can feel the nutrients spread out through my body every time I drink it. I had my first sip of carrot juice when I was seventeen. I made a weird face, but I kept drinking it because I knew it was good for me. It didn't take long before I craved carrot juice and I ended up loving the taste.

One of the big ways of connecting with Spirit is by raising your vibration. Someone who partakes in fortune telling readings, or who is gifted with psychic foresight could have a low vibration or operate from their ego, but they are still able to connect effortlessly. Raising your vibration is much more important in doing beyond reasons of being more psychic. You pick up on heavenly messages when your ego steps out of the way of your higher self. Meditating and being in a still environment in nature is a great way to access Spirit much easier than when you're under stress or any other negative emotion. This raises your vibration and opens up your clair channels, which also gives you more mental alertness and stamina.

Your vibration is an invisible energy field within the DNA of your soul, aura, and body. The ones able to see that the energy is not invisible are those in Heaven. An Earthly soul with a dominate clair, such as clairvoyance, can see the energy field as well. A clairsentient will be able to feel this energy. The vibration energy is always a part of you. It is made up of undetectable cells by the human eye. They fluctuate and change colors depending on your mood, your thought processes, who you surround yourself with, as well as what you ingest into your body. Your soul and entire aura is an everlasting breathing energy field that has an effect on your state of mind. This is whether you desire to be happy in this life or miserable. You can be a CEO who is a perpetual angry curmudgeon that is rude to the staff and only interested in making money in any way they can. This person might be financially successful, but they are still miserable and a spiritual failure. This angry state lowers their vibration, which brings in an onslaught of negative circumstances, and harsh health issues at some point in their life. This is due to the angry stressed state they've endured throughout the course of their human existence. It builds up like mold in a damp basement, until the individual decides to eradicate it and make some healthy lifestyle changes. Doing this can help them be more in tune, which will in turn assist them in building their business to even greater success. In fact, there are a great many business executives who actually consult the Tarot from time to time.

You are in a temporary physical body with an inflated ego that pushes you to anger or sadness when life circumstances throw you a curve ball. This can be inevitable depending on the kind of life you live and who you surround yourself with. You could be a busy professional who works a job that drains your soul's life force. Working a job you despise will lower your vibration. You sit in traffic to get to this job you're unhappy at, only to leave at the end of the day and sit in traffic to get home. This stress in driving in those conditions lowers your vibration. This is why it's vital to incorporate some fun in your life at least one to two times a week. Take frequent breaks throughout the day that include getting outside to breathe in some fresh air. Heavens messages travel along the particles of oxygen, which invigorates your life force.

The fun you inject can be whatever lightens your load. It can be getting together with a friend to go to a restaurant to hang out and shoot the breeze. It can be heading off to the beach or to go on a hike in nature.

It can be watching a funny movie or playing a board game. It can be date night with your lover, or releasing tension at the gym in a workout. Spirit won't point the finger and tell you not to drink a six-pack of beer to lighten that load. That's something only you can decide. Drinking a six pack lowers your vibration and you wake up feeling even more rundown. I know because I've been in that state myself.

Every living organism, plant, animal, element, atom, and cell vibrates of energy. When you take a stroll through a garden or park, you'll notice an invisible heavy weight being lifted off you. You suddenly start to feel elated and more relaxed. This is an example of what it might feel like as your vibration begins to rise. But then you get a phone call from a friend who is a gossip and proceeds to tell you about how someone you both know did something and they angrily disapprove. Now your vibration begins to decline, and you didn't do anything, but answer your phone. You were on the receiving end absorbing the negative energy your friend was outwardly shooting at your soul. Now your vibration has dropped down.

Some animals will dart away when they sense a hostile energy coming towards them. They're so in tune and have a high vibration that they guard their territory without thinking about it. The reason most animals have high vibrations is because they do not live the kinds of lives that human folk live. They're not stressing out over making money to pay rent. They're not falling into emotional turmoil because a lover has left them. They eat, breathe, move, go to the bathroom, sleep, and then repeat.

A pet of an abusive owner will have a dropped vibration. If the animal has been trained by the owner to feel fear due to the poor abuse of that human owner, then the fear emotion drops the vibration. Human souls are responsible for the havoc and destruction that happens on this planet. They're responsible for the harm done to people, animals, planet life, and so on. The other exception is Mother Nature. The weather on the planet can be uncontrollable and erratic in places. It can and will destroy anything in its wake. Earth can thrive and prosper rapidly without humankind tampering with everything.

The astrological sign of "Pisces" is considered one of the most psychic signs in the zodiac, because like the symbol of the fish they are born absorbing every nuance naturally. Like a fish in the water, when you attempt to get close to someone who has "Pisces" in the top tier of their chart, that person will evade or swim away. You have to keep at them if you truly care to ensure they know you're safe to be around. Feeling every nuance causes heavy burden on the backs of the Pisces. They can be prone to addictions to hard substances just to get rid of that feeling. When they evolve and become more aware that it is a gift and not a curse, they can reach greater heights than anyone has ever dreamed of. We're using the sign of the Pisces as an example in order to demonstrate what it's like for someone who might have strong sensitivities and how they might navigate through life. This is regardless of what someone's sign is. Will it be addicted? Or will they choose to soar high above the clouds?

When you welcome the hostile energy in someone else, then you become one with it. Others will go along with whatever the person is complaining about to them. This drops their vibration. You might have a complicated life and therefore you live in ways that are not conducive to raising ones vibration. Perhaps it's at a cutthroat stressed out environment at your job, or with your home life. This is about being aware of what can and will lower your vibration, while doing your best to avoid the negatives when possible. When your mind is consciously aware of what you need to do even when you're not doing it, then this is a step in the right direction. It becomes second nature to you as you adopt healthier life changes.

I'm a lifelong addict and a former obsessive compulsive mess. My most addicted years were in my late teens to early twenties. I was drinking tons of alcohol, doing lines of cocaine, meth, smoking cigarettes, and marijuana regularly. As I was doing that, I was consciously aware in the back of my mind that if I'm not going to stop, then I better incorporate some healthy lifestyle choices. I'd do a line of cocaine and chase it down with carrot juice. This lasted until I started following my Spirit team's guidance. I was listening to them during that time, but I was ignoring them like a spoiled child ignoring his parent's naggings. My Spirit team has always been igniting my inner life force to the point where I would crave toxic vices less to complete elimination of the toxic addiction. I knew I needed to stop, so I eventually folded and requested their help in doing so.

My Spirit team says that alcohol in high amounts lowers your vibration. This does not mean that they are demanding that you stop drinking. Your choices to do, stop, dissolve, or reduce particular life choices that drop your vibration is for you to decide. If you enjoy drinking a bottle of wine every night and yet you regularly question why you're not content with your life, and nothing ever goes your way, then this would be one of the possibilities as to what is blocking what you desire from entering the picture. Since alcohol in high amounts blocks the divine and lowers your vibration, then you miss out on the messages and guidance from your own Spirit team.

Some of the common messages and guidance I've received from Heaven are geared towards the importance of exercise and taking care of all things connected to your body. I've been into physical activity since I was a kid thanks to the urging of my Spirit team. Even when I fell off the wagon and into heavy toxic addictions, such as drugs, cigarettes, and alcohol as a late teen and young adult, I was still greatly aware of the importance of taking care of myself in the back of my mind. My Spirit team dominated my need to destroy my body and got me back into shape by focusing strongly on my overall well-being by the time I was around twenty-five years old.

Raising your vibration is a lifestyle change that needs to happen over time for your soul's benefit and not for anyone else's. There are values that need to be adopted or modified in order to reach a centered place that helps you be more connected. If you're obsessing daily for months over an ex-lover who is no longer in your life, then this is a block that lowers your vibration. This ex has left you, moved on, or perhaps blocked you on social media or on a phone app with no explanation, yet you cannot find a way to let it go and move on. This lowers your vibration. You are checking your ex's social media page regularly to see what they're up to. Are there signs they might be interested in you again? Who are they talking to? What photos do they post with other people in them? Could they be romantically or sexually connected to any of the people in the photos? What about those who comment on your ex's posts? Is something going on with your ex and that commenter?

This is your ego desperately curious to know or find out some clues about what's going on with this ex lover. This lowers your vibration and creates a block. If someone is no longer interested in communicating with you, then that is your cue to work on moving on. I understand this as I've been there too. Talk to a counselor, therapist, healer, or join a support group and get out more and connect with friends. Find ways to muster up the effort to continue on with life without them. It will be a struggle, but overtime it will get easier. The thoughts of them will dissolve gradually to the point where it's only once in awhile. And even at that point, the emotional quotient surrounding the thoughts won't be as intense as they once were.

The moment you visit this person's social media page to spy and read their posts with the intention of discovering new information that can benefit you, then your vibration drops. This isn't about checking a friend's page to see what they've been posting lately to find out what they're up to because you've been busy with work, school, or any other life activity. You don't have any emotional interest except genuine positive feelings to stay up to date on your friend's life. That will likely not lower your vibration unless you read a tirade of negative posts from them.

A low vibration is what makes you depressed, miserable, angry, or agitated. When you focus heavily on this ex, talking about them, focusing on it, and wondering, then this drops your vibration. Your vibration continues to drop every time you obsess over their every move. It's natural to be going through all of those feelings, thoughts, and emotions after a breakup, but eventually you do it less as time progresses on. If you do not, then after a year of this you find that it has ultimately destroyed your life force. This includes your work, friendships, overall soul's well being, and creative pursuits to name a few. It stalls circumstances until you begin the process of re-raising your vibration again and getting back to that place of perfect contentment. You will get there with effort and discipline. It's a gradual progression as you deal with the death of what no longer is in your life to make room for what is. Your interest in the coming and going's of others will decline. You'll notice improvement and positive changes happening steadily as a result.

When your vibration is low it takes effort and work to re-raise it. You can raise it when you decide to move swiftly through making important positive life changes and adjustments to reach a place where you're content again. Somebody who is no longer a part of your current life is not your higher self's priority or concern. You begin to think of them less while diving into living life again.

Take frequent breaks and disconnect from technology and/or hostile people in order to re-center and gain perspective. Sometimes the most in tune person can be too close to the truth to pick up on it. Letting loose releases your soul from the clutches of the burdens of the body. It raises your vibration in the process. There isn't enough fun in people's lives these days and so this is much needed. When you tune into your guides energy, write down any great ideas or dreams you've been thinking of no matter how big or small. It can be positive behavior changes and perspectives you want to begin incorporating into your soul make up. This is guidance being passed down to you in some fashion by your Spirit team. They might instruct you to make a pact to have weekend getaways at least once a month or every two months. It can be a business plan or asking someone out on a date. Incorporate these lifestyle adjustments one-step at a time and notice the positive effects that end up coming out of that.

Chapter Twelve

Cut the Cords and Grounding

There are etheric cords that grow and form between yourself and any object you place your focus on, whether positive or negative. This object can be people, material items, or even your thoughts and feelings. When you become attached to any of those things and it is bathed in negativity, then a cord is formed between yourself and the point of your focus. Clairvoyantly this cord looks like a gasoline hose that is dark, dirty, and wrapped in grey cobwebs. It drains your life force and lowers your vibration, especially if it's negative. Not only do you lose the object of your focus due to the blocks erected as a result of your negative feelings, but it delays you from moving forward and brings in more negativity from other areas. It grows like a wild and unruly fire.

If you have constant disagreements with someone, then your connection with them becomes toxic. This is a sign that it is time to cut the cords between yourself and this other person. No one benefits in going back and forth to rehash an issue with anyone where two people are not compassionately seeing one another's differing point of view. This doesn't only apply to friendships, but rifts on social media between strangers not agreeing over a certain viewpoint. Calling people names because they have a separate view is not going to suddenly wake them up. This lowers both you and the other person's vibration. Constructively explain to someone with compassion that hating anyone who is not like you is more likely to open their mind rather than sending a tirade of attacks. It also raises your vibration because you're coming at it from a place of love.

When you think about someone and your thoughts move to upset, depression, sadness, anger, or any other negative feeling, then you have formed a dark cord to this person. You pine over someone you have interest in, but become dejected when you come to the realization that they're not succumbing to your interest. This is a sign you have formed a dark cord to this other person. No love exists within that cord. This is why it is imperative to have those etheric cords cut.

Cutting cords does not always remove this person, so there is no need to fear that you will lose the person after you cut the cords. The only time the person is pushed away or removed is when your Spirit team knows that this connection is not beneficial to your higher self's goal in any way. In the end, the removal of this person or object is for good reason, such as they might have been abusive. Sometimes you have to walk away from someone you love, because you know that the connection is toxic. There are no benefits for anyone in a connection like that. It endures the drama preventing you both from moving forward in your lives. You do not want ten years to go by when you realize how much time you wasted not letting that person go.

Cut the cords to anyone or anything that is toxic, not of love, or of benefit to your higher self's path. If you're wondering what cords you need to release, then examine the negative emotions you're feeling around anyone or anything. Are you feeling sad, depressed, argumentative, stressed, or angry? Whatever the upset is targeted to is a clue as to what you need to release. Let it all go, release it, or let them go. When you cut the cords and release it, then you open the door that brings in new good stuff! You also feel an uplifting surge of positive energy that raises your vibration.

You can say something like, "Archangel Michael I call upon you now. Please cut the cords between myself and *(name of person, feeling, or material object here).*"

You can call on the Heavenly being or guide that you are most comfortable with. You can call on God to cut the cords. Anyone in Heaven can assist in getting these cords cut. If it's a stubborn issue, then you cut the cords to that object every single day until you intuitively sense that all is well again. If you work or go to school with that one person that rubs you the wrong way, then every morning as you begin your day request that the cords be cut between you and this person. I have been cord cutting forever and have noticed miraculous results because of it.

Follow the cord cutting ritual by asking God and Archangel Michael to shield you with protective white light allowing only those of love to be allowed to penetrate it. Cord cutting and shielding needs to be done daily when desired because the shielding fades after 24 hours. The cords dim depending on the toxic people you come into contact with. It is a lifestyle you're adopting to ensure you travel along your path as serene as possible.

Sometimes you're unaware that you've formed a cord with someone else. When you experience negative emotions over anyone or anything, then you're no longer seeing a situation clearly. The road up ahead is filled with a hazy fog that blinds you from reality. Perhaps you're hoping the object of your affections will return your interest, but none is given. This causes you to feel depressed and upset. A dirty damaging etheric cord has now wrapped around your soul and hooked itself onto this other person's soul. Cutting these cords releases the negativity associated with this cord. You do not need to be around someone who is constantly disrespecting you and causing drama. It's not worth it in the end when there are many wonderful peace loving people in the world.

Cutting cords is a beneficial tool you can utilize daily when it comes to enhancing your soul. Your life could be a busy stress packed one where you're surrounded by energies that contaminate your aura regularly. This is where cutting cords can assist. You can cut cords to a former faith based religion that was toxic to you. Some religious teachings within certain faiths have nothing to do with God. They instill traits in you such as fear, guilt, harm, or low-self esteem. Those traits are dark ego teachings and not God teachings. You can be part of any faith you're interested in delving into. You will draw your own conclusions as to what feels right to you when it comes to what others are sharing. Bringing you closer to God should never be done by making you feel bad about who you are. True, honest, faith based spiritual teachings will have love and compassion with it.

Cutting the cords to family, loved ones, or those who have been close to you are the most difficult cords to cut. You can cut the cords without cutting them out of your life. It's the dysfunction that's cut. Sometimes you have to nip it in the bud and say, *"Enough is enough. It's time to cut the cords to this person or situation. My life is intended to be peaceful and not stressful."*

Grounding

Grounding is the process of connecting your soul to the physical world. You can lose yourself if you float too far upwards into the next plane. While this can be exhilarating, it is helpful to find the right balance between the spiritual world and the physical world. Grounding into the physical world helps you reap the benefits of the material world. This isn't saying to desire an over indulgence in material possessions, but there is nothing wrong with obtaining material necessities for your human survival such as a home, family, food, clothing, car, etc. When you're not grounded, you can be feeling out of sorts, chaotic, anxiety ridden, or unfocused. Grounding helps you balance that out so you're clear minded, focused, and full of life.

In order to ground your soul, find a place anywhere in nature, whether it's a park, beach, desert, mountain, or your own backyard. Connecting with physical nature helps to ground you. You can take a walk through these areas and breathe in deeply and exhale. Ask your Guide and Angel to work on grounding you while strolling through a nature setting. Take your shoes off and allow your body to connect with the Earth by planting your bare feet on the ground. This can be in the sand, on a beach, or on the grass in a park. Visualize white light moving from below the Earth, and up through your feet, then through your body, and out through the top of your head. Take deep breaths in and exhale out any stresses, worries, or cares by releasing it all out into the heavens.

Finding an area with little to no people if possible is extra effective, because you don't have the tampering energies of the noise of the crowds. It's perfectly fine to be with a loved one, or calming friend who is looking to chill out in nature and connect as well. Lean your back up against a tree and allow the Earth's healing properties to work its way through you. Working on a garden outside also helps to ground you. You're moving your spirit light into the Earth's light as you work your hands into the physical world. This merges the physical and spiritual part of you. The key is the contact between the physical earth and your physical body. Both simultaneously connect with your spiritual body and light, which assists in igniting your inner life force.

It is essential to ground and vital for the well-being of your overall health. Grounding is connecting with nature and the physical Earth. It's walking barefoot in nature, or anywhere the Earth can touch your skin, such as the woods, grass, lake, or beach. Grounding is helpful in obtaining a stronger frequency connection with your Spirit team. It's more than just putting your feet on the soil. It's planting your feet on the ground while sitting or standing. Close your eyes and feel and visualize tree roots wrapping around your feet and growing downward into the ground. Take at least a few minutes or longer if you prefer to do this.

There have been scientific tests conducted on individuals who were considered to be unhealthy. The test required them to go barefoot in nature to connect to the physical Earth. They used an infrared test that revealed them as they grounded. It revealed that before they began grounding, the cells in their body were dark. As they grounded, the dark cells lightened and showed fewer of them in the test subject's bodies. This isn't surprising since all living souls and organisms are made up of cells and energy that is constantly shifting depending on your lifestyle and those you surround yourself with.

Grounding assists in giving you a stronger connection with the other side. Close your eyes, inhale deeply, and then exhale. Do this exercise several times until you feel relaxed. Then, as you're continuing to inhale, imagine you are inhaling bright white light. As you inhale this light, allow it to move through your body and consume all of you inside and out. Exhale breathing out this light so that it is surrounding your body and growing larger. You might feel a little dizzy or lightheaded while grounding and connecting. This is releasing toxins out of your body and replacing it with Heavenly light. You are having high psychic input where it's bouncing all over the place. This is whether or not you hone it or take classes to keep the hypersensitivity at bay. Grounding can certainly help to bring your soul back down to earth. Have one foot in this world and one in the other.

I go into detail on all things connected to your vibration energy in my pocket book, *Raising Your Vibration*.

Chapter Thirteen

Identifying Blocks

It's beneficial to reach that place where you are grateful and thankful for what you have in the moment. It's still a difficult task to accomplish when your soul knows what it desires next and sees no movement. I understand this frustration as I've been there too. What I have desired eventually has come to fruition. One of the many teachings that Heaven has passed down to me is to feel grateful for what you have now. This state of being is what raises your vibration. The raised vibration is what brings in those desires you crave. The feeling grateful condition is of benefit to you because of the rewards that come with it. When you're feeling good, then more of that greatness comes into your life. When you feel lousy, pessimistic, and miserable, then it's as if it's one bad thing after another. This is how the law of attraction works. What you put out is returned back to you, and what you reap, you sow. Plant the seeds of what you want now, and then later watch it blossom into fruitful flowers and come to fruition. These are common metaphors because many have expressed to having tested out these theories with great success.

It is common sense that if you want a job, then you have to fill out job applications, or send out your resume. No one is going to call you with a job offer if they don't know who you are or that you're looking for work. You want to win the lottery, then increase your chances by buying a ticket. These are basic examples of how the universe works. When you put a little effort out there, and you ask your Spirit team for assistance, then they meet you half way. It isn't enough to do all three, but you want to also feel optimistic, excitement, and gratefulness at the same time. Putting all of those traits together is a winning combination that will take you further to success, instead of being perpetually negative, pessimistic, and full of worry.

Whenever I would suggest anything to one client that would change her life, she would respond with something negative. I would hear statements from her ego such as, "Oh, they'll never hire me. They'll want someone thinner or younger." Or, "I'm not qualified." I noticed the repetitive negative words she was voicing. There comes a point when you're helping someone else that you discover they're not interested in changing. This is your cue to begin backing away. There was nothing I could say that would break her out of that monotony. Her lower self and ego was the ruler of her life. This is why she remained jobless and in an unhappy relationship. When in that negative state, the individual is not always putting in the work or asking Heaven for help. How I obtained my past desires we're by asking for help, and following the guidance by putting in the work.

When I was sixteen, I knew I would get into the entertainment business. For the most part I had consistent excitement and optimism about it inside. There were the occasional doubts or worry that I would not get in, but those feelings were rare. They would only pop up once in a blue moon for a minute. It was so infrequent that it did not dominate or rule me. I'd naturally and quickly move right back to optimism and in feeling grateful. I also had it in the back of my mind that I would keep trying until I was 80 years old or dead. I asked my team frequently for assistance in prayer. I paid attention to what they were guiding me to do, and then I took action and followed it. With hard work, passion, and persistence I eventually saw results.

Sometimes the grateful state of mind is experienced by force such as a less than stellar situation takes place in your life where you realize, "Okay, things were better before. Now I wish I wasn't complaining as things are much worse now!" The constant complaining was a block preventing positive movement. Coming across someone who has it far worse than you do is something that can shake someone out of their negative rut. The guilt comes on for having complained repeatedly about how unhappy you are with where you're currently at. No one in Heaven wants to see you unhappy. They do want to help guide you out of it. You're not purposely being ignored since they're not cruel. There are steps that need to be taken to reach that space of happiness.

Guilt is another trait that can block one from success. You feel a twinge of guilt that you are undeserving of good and this creates a block between yourself and your desires. When I was a teenager and attempting to get into the entertainment business, I had the slight guilt that would twitch at me that I was asking for too much. Luckily, those moments were rare since most of the time my basic nature is one of optimism. Guilt also comes onto someone who feels they're being an imposition. Someone who is a sensitive with strong Clairsentient channels might feel guilt when someone wants to help or do something nice for them. It's merely a matter of catching yourself when you fall into a negative state, and then immediately work on shifting your mind's thoughts down a more positive and uplifting direction.

If the guilt were a reaction to how poorly you treated someone else, then you would work on shifting away from the guilt and making amends with the person you treated in a hurtful way. This is by being aware of your surroundings and how you treat others. You pay that karmic debt back by reaching out to that person to bury the hatchet from a place of compassion. You consciously know that you want to make it right. Once that's accomplished you move on to the next level. It sounds contradictory to point out that you should not feel guilt, but you should also not feel nothing at all either, because then you're moving into sociopathic territory. The trick is to find that middle ground where you're aware of how or what you've done to someone, but you're not drowning in the guilt. Nor are you living in a state where you are unfazed by your behavior.

Some circumstances have barriers and blocks that are in the way from you experiencing the life you want. When you've admitted to these feelings, then that is a great step towards reaching the breaking point where you're freed. You become highly aware of what has caused these uncomfortable emotions. You've sacrificed your happiness to do what you feel is right. This is an amazing quality to have, but it's also time to begin the process of thinking of you first. There's nothing selfish about making sure that you're taken care of before anything or anyone else. If you're not taken care of, then it's difficult to take care of anyone else. Others may walk all over you and take advantage of your goodness when you display signs of being totally selfless with nothing in return. They don't necessarily do that on purpose, although some do, which is where one must train them to treat you and others with respect. In general, they are typically not fully aware that this is how they're behaving.

As you remove the barriers that have been erected in front of you on your path, then your Clair channels will begin to work at optimum levels. The negative feelings are creating these blocks. You're applauded by Heaven when you make positive life changes, such as giving up or reducing certain addictions that cause these blocks. Sometimes that's not enough if the negative feelings are still there as that is also a block. This is partially why working on extricating negative thoughts and feelings is equally essential. You have a conscious and you're extremely aware of what's going on around you, so it's challenging to not be paying attention to it, or noticing how you feel.

Unhealthy relationship connections are also a block. There can be some relationship healing that needs to take place. This includes forgiveness, letting go of blame, or any feelings of victimhood associated with a broken connection that continues to plague you. Call on the Archangel Raphael for assistance and ask him to work with you on that daily until all is well again.

Your mind and your body go through a work out with physical human life challenges. It can be super exhausting causing you to feel overwhelmed and stuck. All of these circumstances can create blocks in your way from obtaining good. Know that you do deserve good and are deserving of love.

These blocks can be removed by requesting heavenly assistance. Other ways are by taking frequent breaks each day. This is taking at least fifteen minutes once a day where that time is solely for you. Find an area where it's not crowded with people and take regular walks. It can be to walk around the block, or strolling through a place where you know you won't feel assaulted by any harsh energy emitting off of others. This includes avoiding a busy street with cars racing by. You need quiet in order to contemplate. Doing this will help you to clear your mind out.

Allow your thoughts to wander while on these walks. Your thoughts may start off on the negative side over a circumstance that's been bothering you, or you'll be thinking about where you're at with your life. While being outside and going for those walks, you'll work on emptying all of that stuff out that's distracting and plaguing your mind. This might sound silly initially, but sudden revelations, guidance, and awakenings are received from spirit out of the blue while doing that. Someone goes on their tenth walk and arrives back home with an amazing idea that has filtered through them that was guided by spirit. It turns out to be an answered prayer. Your team can easily work on you when you're not distracted by anything else. Look at every year as another chapter in the book that is your life. Work with God and your Spirit team by communicating with them regularly on how you would like to see your life mapped out. It doesn't matter if you feel that you're talking to yourself or not hearing them. You are heard and eventually the answer will come to realization for you.

Admitting is the first step to recovery. When you've admitted that the way things are in your life are not jiving with what your soul truly desires now, then the closer you are to progress. You are ready for changes and to have things shaken up a bit. It might seem as if you're off track or at a standstill, but in fact, you are very much on track. A standstill feeling is the crossroads point where the inner transformation takes place as you begin to move in the direction towards what you truly love.

The Shift in Consciousness

A good deal of what is taught about the consciousness can come out convoluted. This makes it challenging to understand what is being explained. When there is talk of vibration, frequencies, energy, and consciousness, then this can fly right over someone's head unless it's explained in simplified terms. In the end, the goal is the same where the betterment of humanity is desired. The betterment of humanity starts with you.

(Dictated by Saint Nathaniel,
Translated by the Author)

We cannot willfully deny that there is a shift in consciousness taking place around the world within individual souls. It has been this way since the dawn of humankind. It takes centuries for human souls to evolve. When you examine Earth's history, you will note how long it's taken for life as human souls know it to be unnecessarily violent, negative, and filled with hate. This is still going on today and to deny that is to live naively. While we insist and urge one to display love whenever possible, the state of humanity is chaotic. This disorder is what will break the dam that allows a shift in consciousness. This madness has been going on throughout Earth's history. As the population of human souls has grown, so has pandemonium.

When you experience constant discomfort internally with amplified emotions, this may feel to be connected to a shift in consciousness. While this is true to an extent, it is more multifaceted than that for us to place a label on it. Humankind desires labels in order to understand circumstances and people in a broader way. The negative side to labels is when you use it to create separation from one another. Any negative feelings prolonged in you can have a variety of factors attributed to it. These factors and effects are connected to the way humankind has designed Earthly life with its structures and rules. While having structure and discipline is important to a degree in order to minimize chaos, it also creates havoc depending on how restricting you are with others.

Someone who is experiencing prolonged discomfort internally may have developed this at the hands of other people, their surroundings, the boom and noise of technology, lack of exercise, poor diets, and lifestyle choices. These are some of the potential major contributors towards these turbulent feelings. Forcing one into a corner experiencing these symptoms does and can contribute towards that soul having a shift in consciousness. A great awakening or shift in consciousness happens with a human soul when they reach a breaking point at some moment in their life. They come to realize that human life and the negativity that exists globally or within their personal life does not make their soul happy.

They begin asking the bigger questions such as, "Why am I here? Why does this place exist? There is nothing but anger, chaos, hate, judgment, unfaithfulness, and so on…" Someone hurts another and that soul's ego feels scarred as a result. They cannot understand how someone can do something to be so cruel to another and feel nothing. Someone who feels nothing and acts out violently towards another is someone without consciousness. They have an aloof detachment from their soul and everything beyond the physical reality they've created.

You asked about 12/21/12. We've spoken before about the Mayan Calendar and its effects or non-effects long before December 21, 2012, which was the day that humankind believed to be the end of the world. The reason we've never gone any further in depth is because there is nothing to talk about. This was a fad that caught on around the globe and has no bearing on anything legitimate. We said, "December 21, 2012 will come and go like any other day." The day did come and go with no noticeable shift.

The talk began to build in 2012 as you moved closer to 12/21/12. The Mayans did not make any sort of prediction that the end of the world would be on this date and nor was a shift intended to take place at that time. The reason the Mayans ended the Calendar on December 21, 2012 is because they were invaded by others outside of their tribe and therefore were forced to abandon the Calendar project.

Human ego loves to hype up drama and with that comes temporary excitement or fear energy that the end is near. The ego also enjoys capitalizing on fear for personal gain. There were movies and books put out about the year 2012 and its significance, as well as for entertainment. If you research history throughout the years, you'll discover that there has always been some measure of apocalyptic scare talk every year. This talk is born out of fear. Fear is connected to the ego.

In some circles, they turned this fear energy into something positive, such as December 21, 2012 being a day where a global shift would take place and usher the universe into a new era. A new era has occurred periodically over the centuries regardless of the Calendar date. This happens as humankind evolves at a slow rate towards the realization that your soul's life is and should be about love. It is not about pushing others down, bullying, or creating a structure of life that contributes to long-term stress, unhappiness, or death. Love is what thrives and carries on indefinitely. Love feels good to your soul. It uplifts and adds a euphoric feeling of joy and peace to your life. Love blasts away negativity and heals the soul. It empowers and contributes to helping the soul achieve greater heights of consciousness.

There was a tragedy that hit the news on December 14, 2012 that involved a young man going on a shooting rampage in Connecticut. There was another shooting just days before that at a mall in Oregon. This prompted some to believe that it was somehow related and connected to "doomsday" on December 21, 2012. Those acts were committed by the free will of people who were not mentally balanced and should have been given help, but were ignored. When you're disconnected to your soul and anything outside of the material world, then you grow oblivious to the signs where someone is in desperate need of love or intervention.

The world is currently shifting for the better and has been for some time. This is where the light is equal to the dark, but that did not have anything to do with the year 2012. What has been happening over the course of the 20th Century and beyond is a global shift. In the 2000's, you moved into high noon where the dark energy in human souls became equal to the light. This means that there are an equal amount of good and light in ratio to the darkness and hate in all human souls. This is witnessed in the human politics arena where you find people seeking and desiring to interfere and control how another person chooses to live their life. This global shift began to accelerate during the 1900's and onward. As the decades progressed, there were more souls being born to usher in this shift with the goal of raising ones consciousness. Many are becoming more aware of their surroundings and how they behave in their life. They are also living in the heavy density of the Earth's atmosphere and not aware of whom they are deep down beneath the physical.

As Earth's history continues, there will be newer generations of souls entering a lifetime in a more evolved manner than the previous generations. This is helped along by the current generations who are evolving and passing it down the bloodline. The 2000's and beyond saw the true beginnings of the rise of the technology age. The positives are this is what can and has contributed positively to the growing consciousness in others. Information is readily accessible and spread much quicker than it ever has. Some of it is bad, but some of it is also good. This is all part of the shift in consciousness.

The dark and light in humankind are battling with one another. While this has always been the case, it feels extremely heightened to you because there are billions of people that inhabit the planet. The way everyone is able to communicate is instant, but this adds coldness to that soul and the globe. This coldness does not contribute to a rising of one's consciousness. Connections with one another are short lived and others behave ruthlessly for personal selfish gain. Humankind is struggling to survive and living under immense stress. This does not contribute to a rising of one's consciousness. This creates an overabundance of unhappy, distant, stressed out human souls trying to survive day to day. Their lives feel empty without any excitement. They reach for time wasters or toxic addictions to keep going. This slowly kills that soul's life force, which does not help in shifting their consciousness. There will need to be a massive uproar, anarchy, and outcry that the way human life is currently designed no longer works. You are becoming hip to the truth that you cannot suffocate the soul.

The shift in consciousness can be seen by the way others live and the positive energy they exude. A deeply spiritual person who is evolved might soon find work or a life purpose that enables them to feel this joy around the clock. They will set up life in an area on the planet that isn't overcrowded with angry, cold, stressed people in a big city. When they live in this recommended design it can make them believe there is a shift in consciousness, but they are disconnected from the hostility that plagues the planet overall. They are no longer in the trenches of that. This can give them the illusion that humankind is shifting in consciousness. We do not deny that many souls are evolving in a rapid way. There is a shift in individual consciousness, but globally that is not the case and will not be for some time. It may be centuries before this is seen on a grander scale.

Half the world despises anyone who does not agree with them or who is of another gender, race, political affiliation, sexual orientation, religion, and so on. These are labels you created that have no connection to the souls reality in the end. If you want to examine if you are globally shifting in consciousness, then visit media websites and what people type on it. This will give you a taste of where you are at with a shifting in consciousness. Many still hate others who they consider different from them. The true spirit within the physical human body has not evolved and expanded above the soul's ego. The ego part of them will make it known verbally or physically that they dislike you. This acting out is not someone whose consciousness is being raised. It is the ego living in fear of others who refuse to live the way it does. This ego has a tantrum like a spoiled child. Those creating this harm are waking other souls up who have been asleep and who have not evolved into a higher consciousness of love, joy, and peace. It is waking them up to realize that how others are being treated is wrong and not of God. The human ego has a challenging time with coming to terms in understanding that God created people differently, but in the end you are not different. You are souls prevented from raising your consciousness by not displaying one act aligned with love and compassion.

Shifting your consciousness is having an understanding that you are here for the purpose of love. You are here for your soul's growth. You are here to evolve your soul as either student or teacher, or leader or follower. You have a detachment to the physical. This means you do not identify with labels such as any race, nationality, man, woman, republican, democrat, gay, straight, spiritual, atheist, nor any other label that limits your soul and places you in a box. You are not your job, the clothes you wear, the house you live in, the car you drive, the family you were born to, the physical appearance you work on to attract or feel good about yourself. These are all fads created by humankind to disillusion you into believing that this is who you are.

Raising your consciousness is coming to terms with this design that has duped humankind into believing that you are something if you have or identify with any of these material physical properties. Labels were created by humankind in order to separate souls from one another, but in the bigger reality it is not who you really are.

Raising your consciousness is moving into the space of love for all. It is accepting that you are a soul in a physical body. You love and appreciate all aspects of you. It is to know that hurting, harming, or hating anyone is to not understand who and what you are. To be a constant complainer lowers your vibration and prevents you from shifting your consciousness into love.

You will become submerged into the physical human life with its ever-changing fads and traditions. This can confuse someone into believing that this is who they are. The shifting in consciousness is being aware of this and not being naïve to believing this is the soul's reality. It is the only reality you know at that particular time in your life due to how you were raised. It was taught by the generations passed. When you recall incidents in your life from when you were five, six, or seven years old, it will feel as if you're watching a movie about someone else. If it was a wonderful time, then you feel nostalgic and miss it wanting to re-create it in your later years.

As human souls continue to evolve, they will begin the process of passing a love mantra around to their offspring and so forth. The ones who have failed at this are the ones who have trained their children to hate or harm others who are different from them. In that respect, this shift in consciousness will take time since it is a generational shift in consciousness that is happening. This has progressively been going on since the beginning of humankind.

There is a war between the light and dark. Those of the light are the ones with a higher consciousness and the dark being the ones attempting to stop that from happening. This is seen all around the world as humankind attempts to assert itself through the darkness of their ego. If one wants to see how things are changing in a way that benefits this shift in consciousness, then look back through history. How long did it take for women to be treated and considered equal? How long did it take before humankind stopped treating blacks as slaves? How long was it before someone who identifies as gay was able to marry someone they love? How long did it take before religions accepted other religions? How long did it take for certain circumstances to happen if at all? You can note that some of these situations you've set up have slightly improved, but it took centuries to come about and even still it's not widely accepted by human ego despite what your laws suggest.

These examples are to illustrate what it means to shift your consciousness globally. While it appears this is beginning to improve and speed up, it will take awhile longer to reach that place of peace on earth. Earth is a ticking time bomb and many human souls are now waking up in larger numbers to the idea that the negative way you treat one another is the real sin. Having this awareness is where the true shift in consciousness resides.

When you do not exude and display love and compassion, then you do not know God. When you step through the gates of Heaven, it is an overflowing love you experience that never lets up. Love is the reason you are here. Love is the answer to the big questions you have about why you are here and why everything was created. It was in order for the soul to learn to love and experience love. When you love any soul, only then are you closer to that goal. All circumstances and paths are connected to love and lead to love. Whenever you're in doubt, bring your soul back to this space of love that lives deep within you even if you have forgotten that it ever existed. You were born from love, you entered an Earthly life from love, and you are made up of love. Nothing else matters in the end, but love.

Think For Yourself
Even If You Stand Alone

Secrets reside in the dark, but they burn up and disintegrate when they hit the light. When the truth is illuminated, then release is experienced. It can be difficult for someone to accept or hear the truth, but you cannot live in denial or in a lie either. Holding onto secrets is a harsh heavy vibration that can only be contained for so long before it bursts out uncontrollably. It'll assault anyone who happens to be in that line of fire. Use compassion when revealing a long held secret and ensure that you are safe from harm, since those who operate in a lower energy space are rarely able to accept your truth. It is threatening to their ego and they might react in ways that are inappropriate or harmful.

Many young people live in self-doubt and insecurities. They are at times growing up in areas where there is no support system. Their parents and teachers are telling them what to do, how to feel, what to think, who to follow. They might not feel as if their own friends love them unconditionally. They feel they have to pretend in order to believe they are part of the group. They feel disconnected and isolated due to not being loved, understood, accepted, or heard. You question God's existence and your own mortality. Be your own seeker of truth, do your research, and ask the bigger questions to come to your own conclusions that make the most sense to you. This is your life and in the end no one owns that life, but you. This does not only apply to young people, but it also pertains to adults who have grown up in similar circumstances. When it's left unmanaged, you grow into adulthood and witness these same issue patterns and experiences following you around indefinitely.

Spiritual teachings in the school system are sadly lacking in most classrooms around the world. Incorporating basic spiritual teachings in the classrooms is a step in the right direction to improve and lift up humanity. Change starts with the individual soul. If the individual soul does not change, then the world and humanity will not change. No ruler or government can fix those issues if the souls in humanity are dead. Once you reach a certain age, beyond your twenties, you're mostly set in your ways and there is very little that can be done. This is why you begin spiritual practice lessons in grade school.

The young person is still a sponge absorbing everything around them. Mathematics, History and Geometry is great, but that doesn't teach you anything about the basics in navigating through one's life effectively on a day-to-day basis. There is an excess of issues and disorders that people battle with everyday. Most of the time others are the cause of this since you are not born with disorders such as social anxiety, although some disorders are genetic predispositions like depression.

Someone behaves inappropriately, badly, or without basic common compassionate class etiquette and this affects everyone around them. When it affects the same person repeatedly it brings them down. It becomes a struggle for them to lift themselves back up while in the presence of harsh toxic people. You start popping pills to function, feel better, and get through it. Or you resort to addictions to alcohol, drugs, or bad foods. You become hardwired with the disorder unable to move through life unless you're on something.

If people were trained early on with basic spiritual principles, there would be more love and compassion in the world. It is irresponsible parenting and teaching to not incorporate basic spiritual principles, which include proper etiquette to function in society as a decent person. If human souls kept their ego in check, there would be peace on Earth. No wars, fighting, hate, or causing others pain. It would be as if you were back in Heaven where those negative factors do not exist. This is why it is called Heaven, because it is a dimension where the soul experiences pure bliss. It has no desire for negative features in that environment.

Alena, a teacher and parent in Pezniok, is a Wise One and Warrior of Light who incorporates spiritual teachings in her classroom. She says, *"Conscious parenting is one of the main tools to make peace on Earth happen and it works! Teaching Children about their true essence, energy, and how to use it is fundamental in this case. If parents aren't aware enough and cannot be a role model to their child, then the schools definitely should. Such teachings should be the main part of any school curriculum. I've tried this with the kids I've been lucky enough to teach and it definitely has a positive impact on them! The bottom line is it teaches them to be responsible for themselves. It also makes them understand the interconnectedness of everything. From this point of view, taming their ego comes naturally."*

Young people wrestle with and fall into many challenges such as bullying, temptation, speaking harmfully against others, God, peer pressure, social media, drugs and alcohol, religions, sexual attraction to the same sex, loneliness, and isolation. These are only a handful of issues out of much more that need to be addressed through proper parenting and teaching. You do that with an open mind by allowing the young person to follow their own path as long as it's not hurting anybody.

Bullying

With the rise of social media, bullying has been more prevalent than ever before. It doesn't just happen to young people, but adults bully one another too! Bullying is inappropriate behavior that needs to be tackled immediately through disciplinary action if it is happening under the guidance of a Parent or Teacher. Some look at discipline as something negative, but you discipline to correct bad behavior, otherwise the soul never learns or evolves. Disciplining includes getting to the root cause of why the bully is bullying in order to address it and correct it.

Sometimes a bully intimidates someone else that was bullying another to begin with. The person acts out and is labeled a bully. When parents and teachers are in tune, then they're readily able to hone in on what is propelling the bully to act out in order to talk it through. You cannot ignore something and hope it will go away. You have to face it and fix it. This includes those who join in with the bully who initiates a bullying action. This person is a follower and not a leader. They are someone who follows the bully because it's safe to stand and hide behind the bully and join in rather than stop it from happening. All souls must be taught to love and accept all people no matter what. It must be taught in the school systems and at home that it is unacceptable behavior to bully anybody.

Young people bully others because they may not like the person for no reason at all. Or the person they're harassing is considered different in their eyes. The person they're bulling reminds them of who they are deep within. This makes them uncomfortable because they do not like themselves, so they resort to shoving the other person around, or calling them a name.

Bullying is barbaric, improper, and intolerable conduct. It can be someone who aggressively and poorly attempts to assert ones power over another. They'll do this until they are confident that the other person feels belittled and efficiently discriminated against in their eyes. All souls desire love deep down. To single someone out and mistreat them is one of the biggest sins you can commit. The person doing the bullying hasn't been taught proper decorum by a parent, teacher, or even their own friends. They must be taught that aggressively bulldozing over someone is not how you get your point across. This is something schools do not teach and yet it is a valuable lesson that carries that soul throughout their entire life.

Use assertive compassion when you communicate to others. Avoid those who attempt to intimidate or bully you. Let someone of authority who you trust know if this is taking place. Bullying is classless and the result of someone operating from their dark ego. Inside they feel incredibly small or inadequate with insecurities. They counteract that through bullying aggression. Someone who feels big within has no desire to push anyone down because they're already on top of the world. Bullies do not have the common sense tools to deal with the life around them and must be trained and taught. You teach people to respect you and others. Bullies might behave the way they do to exclude others from a group typically out of jealousy or envy. A bully lives in fear, but that fear is translated into aggressive bulldozing and intimidation. They fear that someone else might take something away from them or be better than them. They mask hidden issues that are deeper than the reasons for their bullying behavior. When someone uses less of the dark side of their ego, they will see one who is different and who achieves greatness as someone to admire, appreciate, and aspire to be. It is against God's law to bully any soul in any form. This is part of the hurt, harm, and hate traits that are considered a sin in Heaven.

Bullying is a desire for power and domination. Often times the bully hasn't been properly coached enough to function compassionately and maturely. This is where parenting and teaching comes in. If one chooses to be a parent or teacher in their lifetime, then it is their duty and responsibility to ensure that young people are trained early on about love and compassion for all. To not do so is irresponsible. There are cases where they are doing all they can do, but are unable to control the child. This is where medical or professional assistance should be considered.

There is a difference between the parent and teacher doing their best to illustrate these concepts as opposed to someone just not bothering out of rebelliousness or naivety. This also points to the bully learning this behavior pattern at home or from their friends. People who allow it to go on without correcting it are the ones surrounding the bully. The bully learns this etiquette from somewhere.

Adults who bully others are the result of growing up in an environment where they were bullied. They were in a home situation that did not support or adopt spiritual teachings into their lives early on. Incorporating spiritual concepts include basic human etiquette such as showing compassion and love for all including self-love. You're not belittled by others or made to feel that something is wrong with you when basic spiritual ethics are brought in to your life.

Temptation

Young people are lured into temptation everyday due to inexperience. They might not know or understand the consequences that result out of being tempted. This includes being tempted to gossip with others, drink alcohol, try drugs, have sex, cause harm on someone, and so forth.

Despite what some believe, God is not the one tempting you in order to test you. You test yourself plenty enough that there is no need for Him to do it. The tempting comes from the dark side of human ego. God does not interfere with your free will choice unless you have asked Him to intervene in your life. If you're hanging around your peers or friends you've chosen, and they are trying to get you to do something you're uncomfortable with, then this is not of God. They do not have your best interests at heart. This is that person's ego not hearing you when you are telling them that you're not comfortable with whatever is being dangled in front of you.

Being tempted is a way to teach someone common sense. It is being able to tell the difference between right and wrong. "Right" is doing something that does not cause harm, but empowers you. "Wrong" is something such as engaging in drugs due to temptation. This will cause an array of problems in your life. Drugs are dangerous and will destroy you, your body, as well as those around you. You will lose friends, drive, success, love, and a true passion for life.

I engaged in heavy drugs and alcohol in my late teens to early twenties. I knew while I was doing it that it was not good for me, but I didn't care. I know what it's like to be addicted, angry, and tempted. I fell into that path to escape the pain of the life I was living at the time. I grew up in an abusive household that ultimately and permanently destroyed my spirit causing me to split off into many selves. This resulted in me driving down the many roads of various addictions. I knew I would need to pull myself up by my bootstraps in order to survive. With the help of God and my Spirit team, I began the process of strengthening my soul, dissolving my addictions, and doing my best to focus on what is most important. I brought me back to life with their help.

When you feel you're being tempted to do things that you know do not feel right, then ask your Spirit team and God to empower you, and help you to stay on your higher self's path.

I go into detail of addictions and abuse and how I overcame that in my book, *"Reaching for the Warrior Within."*

Religion

Young people grapple with the idea that there could be or not be a God that exists. They might have been turned off by the concept, or grown confused with it due to hearing negative religious doctrine that seems so farfetched and harmful to their consciousness that they lose any faith they had to begin with. They grow up in households that imply something is wrong with them. This is your life and you must live it for you. You are your own barometer of what feels right. God means many things to different people. He does not judge you, since that comes from the human ego. Your best qualities are pieces of Him. He loves all and will not cast you out into fire and brimstone because you've done something that you feel guilt about. This does not mean that God or any soul being on the Other Side supports and condones those who harm, hurt, or hate others. He expects that soul to grow up, mature, learn, evolve, and work on becoming a better person. Any high vibration soul desires that, including those living an Earthly life.

I grew up enjoying my experiences with the Church. I was going alone at age ten long after my family was because I enjoyed it. I never came across anything that was close to what you hear about today, and the cruelty that is associated with religions and churches. Organized religion has messed up a great deal of people in the world. This has caused them to grow up and live unfulfilling lives because of the disorders and neurosis they've inherited as a result of teachings that train one to believe they are sinful. The individual is repressed with no room for trial and error. They were unable to find their true self, and ultimately grew to have a disconnection from God or anything that resembles religion.

The differences between spirituality and religion are vast with some similarities, and then there are other areas that are not aligned. Those that despise both interchange them as if they are the same, which they're not. Religion has sadly alienated and pushed people away from all forms of a belief system to no belief. It's moved them from one extreme to the other. Organized religion takes no responsibility for the damage it caused in this world as a consequence.

Spiritual doctrine trains you to be responsible for the negativity you place on someone else and on yourself. Those that broke away from organized religion to no belief at all just assume, "All of its bad stay away." When in reality some non-believers incorporate spiritual principles in their lives anyway. They're just not equating it to the "spiritual" label or don't realize that they are indeed spiritual. They do not have a greater understanding of spirituality, and all of its facets, compartments, and possibilities to know they are already doing the work.

Peer Pressure

One of the biggest offenders in tempting young people comes from their own peers. An example of peer pressure is, "If you don't have a drink of this beer, then you are a..."

Your own peers and friends will pressure and intimidate you into doing something you do not initially want to do. They push you continuously until you go along with it. You conform to be liked and to fit in. You are already liked and loved around the clock free of charge by God, your Spirit team, and all in Heaven.

You are here now living this life for the purpose of your soul's growth. Your Spirit team understands that it will not necessarily be easy. You will get beat up a bit to get a little street smart. You will fall into temptation and peer pressure. Both of which are not exempt when you become an adult. Those who fall into this kind of pressure are battling with low self esteem, or feel isolated, and unloved. They might go along with the peer pressure just to be part of the group. They misplace the attention they are getting for real friendship. You're so excited that someone is talking to you that no attention is paid to the fact that they're only talking to you in order to get you addicted to something bad.

Someone with high self-esteem is comfortable with being alone. They're not interested in following the herd in order to be appreciated. They already feel appreciated and loved naturally. This is a feeling conjured up through your strong connection with God. This makes you confident, self assured, and turned off when someone is pressuring you into doing things you're not interested in, or that feel wrong to you.

Do not be afraid to tell someone where you stand or that you're not interested in something. Understand your own moral compass and what things in life feel wrong to you. It can be drinking alcohol, drugs, sex, gossip, or bullying. When you stand your ground many will learn to respect you. If they continue to harp on you, call you names, disrespect you, or harass you into doing something you do not want to do, then this person is not a true friend. Nor is it someone that you should be associating with.

Real friends and good people will respect you and your choices. They accept your decisions to not partake in something that displeases you. Pray for intervention if you find that you're in situations with people that make you uncomfortable. Ask your Spirit team, Heaven, or whomever you're contented to connecting with to step in and help. Tell them your feelings and that you are experiencing being pressured by your friends and circle to do things you're not comfortable with.

Drugs and alcohol are addictions that effect people of all ages from teens to adults. No one is exempt from the temptation to drugs and alcohol. Some teens may experiment with drugs and alcohol and then move on from it, while others will do more than experiment. They will become dependent on it resulting in an addiction to harder substances. They end up being a lifelong addict at battle with it, unless the addiction ends up cutting their life short. Addictions to drugs and alcohol cause an array of irreparable health issues over time. They damage your relationships with those who love you. They also cause detrimental accidents and poor decision making that can destroy your life. The same people who fall into the trap of peer pressure have a higher rate of falling into addictions to drugs and alcohol. This includes someone suffering from depression, low self esteem, as well as loneliness.

Young people are pressured into trying the endless array of dangerous toxins to fit in and be accepted. Many of them don't really want to do it, but they go along with it to be part of the group and avoid getting bullied. This leads to a lifelong battle with addictions. There are many cases where the teachers and parents are to blame. Teens have talked about how they have informed their teachers when things like this happen, but the teachers do nothing.

Social Media

Social media is great in bringing others together, but it is also used as a device for bullying, narcissism, low self-esteem, and speaking harmfully against others. Young people have been targets for predators and bullies on social media to the point where it has pushed them to tears and in other cases taking their own life. Adults are no different since they sit online all day spewing negative harmful words at other people. Often they're much worse, since the younger generations still see the world with some measure of compassion.

This is the life humankind created where everyone wants to be popular, worshipped, and loved. They spend most of their life trying to obtain love and attention from others to feel good about themselves. They jump up and down when fifty people "like" their sexy photo. Does it really matter that people like you? You can live your entire life trying to get that small measure of attention that feeds your ego for a couple of days, but then it goes away and you have to start all over again. It will continue to go away until you become comfortable with you, and who you are inside and out. You realize you're not driven to have others like your posts or tweets.

When you view the behavior of the human condition on social media from a higher perspective, such as Heaven's view, then you can see how ridiculous and absurd it appears. Those who have discovered this nonsense have said, "I think I'm going to be closing my social media account for awhile." They realize the only thing that matters are the real in-person relationships they have.   Who you are on the surface does not matter. You can post seven hundred different selfies, and that is still not who you are. Who you are is who you are inside.   It is what you do and contribute positively to the world. Posting various selfies all day long exacerbates ones low self esteem, and desire for admiration and attention. What you do and contribute beyond that is what determines your worth.

Emulate the real heroes and inspirations in life. These are not the pop artists, celebrities, actors, or reality TV stars of your time. These are the real heroes such as Malala Yousafzai, a young teen girl who was shot in the head by the Taliban. She survived the bullet that went through her head, neck, and shoulder. The terrorists didn't approve of her being an activist for increasing education opportunities for young girls.

After Malala recovered, she continued on with her fight to increase education and raise awareness. This is someone to admire and follow, not a pop star who wears interesting colorful outfits. The ego would rather distract you by getting you to obsess over what a celebrity is doing rather than over the magnificent contributions made for humanity that a young Pakistan girl is doing. The ego is under the illusion that acting in front of a camera or on stage makes someone royalty. Actors and singers contribute joy through entertainment, but there is no need to put them on a pedestal. They are no different than you or I. They just happen to have a job that puts them in front of the camera or on a stage on a regular basis.

When one has low self esteem, suffers from depression, or anxiety, then they are more likely to succumb to the dangers of social media, peer pressure, bullying, temptation, drugs, and alcohol. This is why developing a strong connection with the other side, Heaven, God, and your Spirit team can help boost your self esteem and raise your vibration into a confident radiant love. It is the kind of poise you were already born with. With a strong connection, you can bring that life force out of you again. You'll realize you have less need for addictions and time wasters that only prevent you from experiencing real love. You invest less emotion into your social media accounts because you know it's not real. You no longer take it that seriously.

The positive exception with social media is when one uses it for something constructive that helps others. No one is helped when all you post are your negative feelings about a public figure you hate. That's not worth any attention. People are helped when you post constructive words that can brighten up someone's day. This doesn't mean that you're not allowed to express yourself to get stuff out of you, but understand the consequences and how that not only affects you, but those around you.

It's strange to air ones dirty laundry every second on a social media page. The ego enjoys posting negative words. It enjoys following others that post negativity. It receives a rush high that deceives you into believing that it has any validity. All it does is delay and manipulate you. This lowers your vibration and causes an array of issues in your life.

I've been indirectly called various derogatory names because of my stance on certain issues at times. This isn't news since it comes with the territory of being a Wise One. Two of the biggest topics you never discuss at a dinner party are religion or politics. Trying to shove your views in either category down someone's throat is not going to suddenly give them an epiphany. You're either preaching to the choir or you're not. All it does is contribute negatively to the noise.

Avoid putting out repeated negative attacks on someone including a celebrity, public figure, or political candidate. It is poor form and bad energy that does nothing to help anyone. You do not want to offend anyone who supports someone you don't care for and vice versa. Respect other people's personal choices, until they've disrespected you.

Work hard for what you want rather than waiting for it to be handed to you. Treat everyone the same no matter who they are. This means with respect so long as they're not hurting anyone.

My teachings are empowerment self-improvement philosophies mixed in with heavenly guidance. Move dangerously close to the middle to see all sides. Think for yourself even if you stand alone. Examine issues in grave detail rather than just going along with whatever someone else wants. Do not criticize or insult others, since that is the not thought out point of view. It is mostly not based in truth and will not inspire anybody. Calling someone names comes from the darkness of one's ego.

Loneliness and Isolation

The rise in technology and social media has made others feel higher symptoms of loneliness followed by isolation. Loneliness is an emotional emptiness that you are not loved. You isolate and find it difficult to connect with others in real life "in person" situations. You are isolating if you hang out at home all day avoiding people. Sometimes this is due to shyness, social anxiety, or agoraphobia. You are also isolating if you're finding it easier to chat away on phone apps or social media looking for ways to connect with others. This is typically done with an aloof disconnect. You chat away, but never truly develop a strong in person connection with someone. Technological devices are used to temporarily fill that loneliness void that never goes away until you make your peace with it.

One of my guides calls himself Jeremiah. As I grew into adulthood, he informed me that he is in the "holy book" as a Prophet. As a man living during biblical days, he lived a life of solitude and loneliness. He battled with low self-esteem and insecurities from time to time. He did not fit in with his peers, but he did have a strong connection with God and the other side that strengthened him and his life. This is what made living his isolated life worth it to him. He eventually didn't feel the need to connect with others, since he knew his life purpose was about preaching the word of God. Some have called him, "The Weeping Prophet", due to his high sensitivity to the pain in others.

He said things that were not well received in biblical days, but today are considered Gospel by some. Because he was alienated and ignored by others, this only perpetuated how lonely he felt at times. He was unable to know what it was like to be in a beautiful love relationship as a result of his disconnect from humankind. He was simply too evolved for that time period.

I know and understand what Jeremiah went through as I've ironically gone through similar dealings during certain parts of my life. My connection has always been strong, but a sea of people could surround me and I would still feel disconnected. I knew growing up that I was not like anyone else, and nor did I want to be. This turns away those who are invested deeply in the mediocrity of the material world.

Jeremiah complained quite a bit to God about some of his doubts and sufferings. He wasn't perfect as a Man since no one is. He experienced depression symptoms and felt hated, but he would retaliate in anger about it rather than sulk in sadness. Sometimes ones lonely isolating feelings are a great place to get some perspective on your purpose here. Jeremiah knew his purpose despite feeling lonely and being mocked on occasion. He also complained about the state of the world and his torment of feeling like he was both good and bad. When the low points would hit, then he would be empowered by Spirit in order to carry on with his quest and purpose.

Loneliness is a separating feeling from God, or by being misunderstood by the masses. When your connection is strong, then the lonely feelings begin to evaporate. Jeremiah's connection with God moved in and out over the course of his life as any other highly connected being. To be a great prophet, teacher, healer, or a sensitive will result in being misunderstood. That's just the way it is, otherwise you wouldn't need to be here. This will alienate those who do not understand you. It will result in you feeling lonely and isolated. Whenever Jeremiah would complain about being misunderstood, or when he would experience negative feelings throughout his life, God would tell him, "Attack you they will, overcome you they can't."

When your consciousness is raised, then it's elevated above the others who are not. Someone with a raised consciousness does not misunderstand other people, nor criticize them, unless they did something bad to warrant that. As I grew to know more about my own guides, I discovered the eerie parallels between who they are, and what they've been through if they previously lived an Earthly life, compared to who I am and what I've been through. I eventually said, "I guess that makes sense." I have many qualities both positive and challenging. These are traits the guides too once had to deal with when they lived an Earthly life.

If you've never felt normal, then we say thank God for that. You're special and not like the others. You wouldn't want to have it any other way. People who misunderstand someone is typically due to their consciousness not being raised enough to *see* things clearly and objectively. They have a hard time allowing differing points of view into their consciousness.

There is nothing wrong with desiring love and affection from a friend, family member, or loved one. And if every soul on Earth were trained to express affection and love to all it comes into contact with, then no one would be lonely. Nor would there be constant rumblings and disturbances on Earth. Loneliness stems from feeling as if the world has turned against you the way others did with Jeremiah. But he found strength in his connection with God and in his purpose here. This lifted him out of the lonely feelings that would creep up on him on occasion.

When you feel lonely, then instead of waiting and hoping for someone to hit you up, you send them a hello note. If they're unresponsive, then drop them and reach out to another. Take long walks in a nature setting to get some sunshine, fresh air, and see the beauty around you. Take in deep breaths and allow your imagination to run wild and see the amazing soul that you are.

Sex and Lust

No one was intended to go through life alone, which is why at this time there are seven billion people on the planet. Many have a difficult time committing to someone in a long term love relationship. They have no problem going after someone for sex. Sex is everywhere you look. It's in popular culture, entertainment, music, television, films, books, and online, social media, and phone apps. There's no way to escape from it even if you wanted to.

There is nothing wrong with sex, but the way its viewed now has become terribly unhealthy and distracting. It's no longer sexy, but dull, since there is nothing left to the imagination. People are cruel to one another as it relates to sex. If someone doesn't find you desirable on the outside, then they won't bother talking to you. Others rip through connections and end up living a life of short lived relationships that lack in commitment. To not commit to anything or anyone is done out of fear or ego.

Sex is considered healthy by Heaven, when it is between two people who have strong feelings for one another in a love relationship. Be careful who you merge with physically since you are absorbing their energy as they are soaking up yours. If you connect physically and intimately on any level with someone who is toxic or has a low vibration, then that energy intertwines and latches with yours. If the person is someone who is not spiritual on any level and unaware of vibration raising exercises, then you can absorb that low energy. It can take awhile to remove it from your aura. When two people who have a high vibration make love, then the energy light created is cosmic and out of this world.

Be smart by always using precautions and protection when it comes to all things connected to sex. Investigate and research literature that goes into detail over the repercussions, issues, and diseases that can become a part of you due to one sexual act with another person.

One confusing sexual experience is masturbation. Masturbating is not a sin and nor are you going to Hell if you do it. God gave your human body a healthy sex drive. It was not done so that you could wrestle with the guilt of having partaken in masturbation. What made it wrong were those in society who grew up to view sex as something unhealthy and uncomfortable. This stems back to ancient times where the thinking in those days was governed through fear and not God. Superstitious man made sure that they included it in the holy book that it was a sin. Anything they did not understand, they added to the holy book.

One of my other guides is Matthew, who also contributed to the writings in the holy book. He states, *"You have heard that it was said, 'You shall not commit adultery'; but I say to you that everyone who looks at a woman with lust for her has already committed adultery with her in his heart. If your right eye makes you stumble, tear it out and throw it from you; for it is better for you to lose one of the parts of your body, than for your whole body to be thrown into hell."*

What he meant was hammering home the point of the message Jesus had, which is that if you've thought it in your mind, then you've already done it. This had to do with adultery and cheating. It did not have anything to do with masturbation. It was about someone who is in a committed relationship looking at someone else with lust and how that can drive the person to cheat. This has happened on countless occasions all around the world and throughout history. "Looking" isn't cheating and nor is thinking it, but his beef is that the thinking of something can and has prompted the person to cross over into immorality.

The majority of most of my books to date have touched on these strict views of adultery in one form or another. This comes from an implant into my consciousness from my Spirit team at birth, as it wasn't intentional to be a common themed message through my work. I grew up amongst adultery, which would technically make me a prime candidate as one likely to cheat. I was the opposite of that where I viewed adultery, unfaithfulness, and cheating as reprehensible. It was seen as worse than murder. It was in front of me growing up, and I went in the opposite direction knowing it was wrong. My consciousness is expanded to the point where I wouldn't be able to consciously accept betraying a lover.

The Hell that Matthew was talking about is a metaphorical Hell, since there is no Hell that exists except the one that human souls have created within them. When Matthew was living during those times in history, there was a different perception of circumstances that no longer apply. Be responsible with yourself, with your body, and with others.

Young men attempting to restrain themselves from masturbating find that to be nearly impossible due to the high sex drive they were given that propels them to it. To judge or criticize them for it is silly. It shows that one does not understand the nature of the sex drive man is given by God from an early age. This sex drive eventually dwindles and declines as his human body ages. Those who are wrecked with guilt over having masturbated receive this guilt from those who raised him. Growing up in a devout religious upbringing that considers all things connected to sex as being bad can result in the young person partaking in harmful actions. This means rape, incest, or molestation.

One man was faced with this accusation that came to light in the public eye. He grew up in a strict religious household that viewed all things connected to sex as being wrong. What this gave birth to was when the guy was around the ages of fourteen and fifteen years old. It came out that he acted out sexually in private by molesting four of his sisters repeatedly. Had he been brought up in a household that understood the sex drive of a boy, he would have been more likely to be controlled and not sexually abusive.

Repressing others when it comes to sex because you're embarrassed by it, uncomfortable with it, or you falsely believe that God finds it to be a sin is what causes an array of horrid issues and circumstances as a result. Most of the time these cases happen in households that have an unhealthy view of all things connected to sex.

There is a difference between lust and love. There is nothing wrong with lust as long as it doesn't overtake you to the point where you're unable to function in healthy relationships with others. At that point it becomes one of the deadly sins. It can cause issues at times where it may propel an unhealthy view of sex. You see someone super attractive and your brain sends chemical fireworks that you cannot control. These are your feelings you're experiencing. There is nothing wrong with that pending it doesn't result in you taking action against someone else's will to satisfy that craving. And that it doesn't prevent you from having a healthy long term relationship with someone. Sex with the one you love and are committed to is seen as healthy and beautiful in the eyes of Heaven. This is regardless of one's gender. The hatred that some have towards anyone who is attracted to the same gender is the result of one's upbringing and the lack of a raised consciousness.

Same Sex Attraction/Homosexuality

Having a sexual attraction to someone who is the same gender as you is a common issue that young people wrestle with today. They feel torn and as if something is wrong with them because they have a love crush on someone who is of the same gender they are. The negative feelings they have associated with that are due to the negative words they've heard others utter around them say. People bully others who are different than them by using name calling words such as *gay* or *faggot*, regardless if the person is gay. Society has trained one another to use it as an attack. They can't think of any other word to back up why they despise someone, so they go with the not thought out point of view, because it is all they were taught by their peers. It's like the blind leading the blind. They're just words and have no weight unless you give them validity. This thought process has made those who are gay to be gay-hating too since they don't want to be associated with something that society falsely believes to be a crime against nature. Those who are uncomfortable with same sex attraction view their surroundings in a limited way. Their consciousness hasn't expanded enough to see that it's love like any other. Or perhaps the young gay person lives in a strict religious household that continues to teach false beliefs that being gay is a sin and that there is something wrong with you.

From all of my connections I've had with Heaven since I entered this life, I've never heard that to be the case from God or my team in Heaven before. They've said the opposite when I've asked about it in the past. They don't emphasize or get into same sex attraction much because it's irrelevant to them. They've basically said that it's only a big deal because you've made it a big deal, but it's not. They are happy to hear that a soul has found love with another soul. This is a loveless world to begin with and anything that has love in it receives the thumbs up from God.

When you love another soul, regardless of that person's gender, then you are closer to God. An advanced high vibration soul does not care who someone loves as long as there is love in the equation.

It is about experiencing the love feelings that raise your vibration, and then you have made that connection with God. This is the goal Heaven is after with human souls. To love another person is to know what it's like to be in Heaven and to know God.

Some hear others have distaste towards those who are gay. And then you have young people listening to that and wrestling with strong feelings for someone of the same gender when they shouldn't even be worrying about it. You love someone? Great! At least someone on the planet is experiencing love.

Those who have an issue with it operate from the space of their ego. Only the ego separates others by race, religious interests, political affiliation, or sexual orientation, etc. All souls come from the same place on the other side regardless of how they appear in this life. The way they appear in this life is due to human genetics. Someone who has distaste for another who is homosexual in this life is due to ignorance and not being taught compassion and love for all. These concepts are in the holy book, but it is interesting that those passages are not followed or quoted.

The ego will do whatever it can to push away anybody who is not like them. They will go as far as to believe that God hates anyone who is born into this life as a homosexual. They will quote passages in the Bible that says this, but other than that they quote nothing else. They ignore the passages about adultery, divorce, and love. Understand that man and his dark fearful ego added those homosexual passages at a later date. If it were written to be God's word, then they would've written down something entirely different. God created all souls and He loves all souls without censure. God does not speak in negative words, but uplifting love filled words. The ego writes words of hate.

There are cases where those who have same sex feelings have incarnated from a previous life where they were homophobic. This is in order to get that soul to walk in someone else's shoes, specifically one they once despised. This educates the soul and helps them evolve.

I go into detail on what Heaven thinks about things such as homosexuality, abortion, as well as what happens to your soul when you die in my pocket book, *Divine Messages for Humanity.*

Past Life

This is not the first time souls have lived an Earthly life. Some have had repeated lives even though most may not recall them. When one is experiencing a strong connection, this opens up the portal to who they might have been in another life or what they might have been going through at that time. Others have been able to get visuals presented to them in a flash of who they once were. All of your past lives are connected and this can help in determining what you might have been going through in that past life and how that applies to your life today. Other than that, it does not have much relevance to know this information.

My own personal belief on past lives is on the fence, but as I've stated before, I relay what I'm given by my

Spirit team regardless of what I personally believe. Sometimes what I believe goes hand in hand with them and other times I hang out in the middle open to the possibility without fully going along with something.

<u>Regression Therapy</u>

Regression therapy is a form of psychotherapy where the therapist examines the varying layers of an individual from their conscious mind to their subconscious mind. The therapist has the goal of working with the patient to examine emotional symptoms and how they came about. This could be someone as an adult who was a victim of child abuse. This causes an assortment of emotional disorders they cling to decades later even though the abuse has been long over. The effects carry on into adulthood preventing that person from accomplishing their dreams and living a full happy life.

The therapist hones in on that with the goal of dissolving the emotional disorders as much as possible by working all of that out.

Physical ailments tend to be a product born out of an emotional disorder. The therapist starts with the physical ailment and works its way to the emotional disorder and then works their way into discovering how the emotional disorder came about to begin with.

No one is born depressed or full of anxiety. These are traits that grow out of being brought up in an unhealthy environment. Ones caregiver, peers, community, and society impose this harshness on the child as it is growing up, while other times it can be partially genetic and even diet related. You rarely see a six year old express negativity and hate on a daily basis. This is because they haven't been fully tampered with or wrongfully influenced by their surroundings yet. This corruption happens to many human souls and yet no one considers it to be child abuse. Seeking out some form of therapy and counseling can be immensely helpful in addressing harsh issues you battle within. An objective party can view circumstances in a different way than you might.

Positive Words

The actions, thoughts, and feelings you experience dictate what is to come into your life. This is why it's important to be aware of your body and its senses within and around you. Use positive words and affirmations when you speak, think, or write. These words and affirmations are bathed in energy. When that energy is negative, it brings more of that to you. When it is positive, then it brings more good into your life. You send those words out into the Universe even if you're just thinking it. If you're constantly thinking negative words in your mind or out loud, then this is sent out into the Universe and brings that energy back to you. Suddenly you find one thing after another happening in your life that isn't good. Someone who tends to be optimistic, and uses or thinks positive words, will find that more goodness comes into their life. Their vibration energy is raised and this brings great things and people into their lives.

Be mindful of all that you are inside and out. Be aware of everything that is around you. Understand how circumstances are affected by who you surround yourself with, how you think, feel, or write online, or in a journal. Go it alone if you have to. You have God and your Spirit team by your side. You are more than an army of one. It is better to be alone than to be in connections with those who cause you to feel unhappy or uncomfortable. Stand strong in your own soul and be your own authority. Govern your life as if you are an executive running your own business. This business is your life and must be loved, respected, committed to, nurtured, taken care of, and taken seriously. This translates to how you treat yourself and your relationship connections with others.

My Near Death Experience

I've been hearing the voices of my Spirit team on the other side since I was a child. They've always been talking to me *clairaudiently* through my left ear as if they are in the same room, or standing next to me. They say things to me that have later come true or happened. All through my life they have been working with me, guiding me, and assisting me along my path. They have warned me of danger as they work with me like any teammate or partnership. They have done their best to intervene when I've fallen down the dangerous paths of toxic addictions, or they've guided me to say something out loud that can help someone. I've been talking to my Spirit team daily for as long as I can remember. It is the way you talk to a friend about any issues, concerns or questions you have. They are some of my best friends.

Sometimes they speak to me individually, while other times they communicate in perfect unison and harmony. There were instances where I would tell someone something about themselves prompting them to look at me perplexed, "How did you know that?" Or "That's my Grandmother. She passed away years ago."

When a departed stranger's loved one in Heaven has spoken to me are the times where I was made to believe and understand that the soul does not die. It goes to a place where it is alive, healthy, and beyond happy and content. My Spirit team has been front and center for me helping me obtain any job I've ever wanted from the film business, to writing books, and to everything in between.

When I've needed assistance from them, I've requested their help, and they've come through for me. I have an analytical mind and require proof of things. I have been testing my team out consistently, and they have proven their existence to me time and time again. Working with them has improved my life in immensely beautiful ways that would not have happened had they not been there.

I didn't have a name for my team growing up, but I knew they were not in the Earth plane. I didn't associate a label with them such as Angels, Spirit Guides, Heaven, or the "Other Side". I also didn't know that hearing the voice of spirit was called Clairaudience. I'm seven years old and it's not like this stuff was taught to me in school. I didn't think there was anything unusual about it and I assumed that everyone had the same deal. I learned that this was not necessarily the case. Everyone indeed has similar gifts, but they are not paying attention to it. This is easy to do since there are moments in my busy jam packed life where I'm disconnected or distracted and not listening to my team. Then there are moments where it is crystal clear reception. Sometimes it would happen randomly and other times it would happen when I was exuding a healthy state of mind. Over the course of my life through trial and error, I was able to detect what can or will not give you that strong reception with ones Spirit team. Some have stronger senses than others because they have fewer blocks.

On November 22, 2010, my life changed permanently when I suffered what my Spirit team called a, "near death experience that lasted a millisecond", even though it felt like it lasted for hours. It was the awakening moment when my former selves died and gave birth to someone new, different, and completely awakened. The weeks before that night, I was suffering from an exercise work out injury that turned into an agonizing infection called Epididymitis.

It's a common infection that active men or male sports players aged 20-40 have experienced and therefore understand the pain involved. However, my infection dragged on for three to four weeks of indescribable pain preventing me from moving unless absolutely necessary. I didn't want to go to the hospital as that brought up all sorts of egoic fear in me. The night before I was transported to Heaven, my mother who is Clairvoyant and Clairsentient, had a dream where I had died. She was filled with heavy grief and loss not knowing what to do about it. At that same moment, I was battling this severe work out infection. Every step I attempted to take was met with relentless pain that shot throughout my body.

On the night of November 22, 2010, I finally folded and requested help from Heaven in a prayer. At that moment, I lost consciousness for what felt like hours, but in Earth time was a nanosecond. This loss of consciousness was not due to medication since I was not on anything. This consciousness was also not a full loss since I was partially cutting in and out of reality.

I lay there with my eyes wide open knowing that I was moving into a channel space. I soared out of the darkness and over the clouds that were bursting with light shining through it. Amongst the surrounding clouds were spirits in a physical body, but not a human physical body. They were all standing spread out among the clouds. I traveled past them feeling unusually content and pain free. There were many of these spirits scattered about and I knew who they were.

They were my Spirit team of Guides and Angels as well as other spirit beings from family back home. I rocketed directly towards what looked like an extremely tall lamppost. It was the only object that was dark in the distance. As I moved closer to it, I noticed the light around it growing larger. It was Archangel Michael who towered about thirty feet tall. He said to me, "We're working on it." This was his way of responding that Heaven has heard my prayer and cry out for emergency assistance.

After regaining human consciousness, I discovered I was back in my body lying on my bed. Only now I was ecstatically elated. The consistent sharp pains in my body that I felt for three weeks straight were lightening up. The worst was over and the miracle and healing process had begun. A euphoric high flushed through me and took over. I was seeing things clearer and in ways that I had not noticed much before. I was different, altered, changed, and empowered like a super hero or a super human.

I pinched and touched my arm repeatedly because being back in my body was strange to me. I was aware there was a difference between my physical body and the awakened soul part of me. Without a doubt I knew nothing was going to be the same moving forward.

I interlocked my hands and placed them over my head. A download of endless data, messages, guidance, and information was being uploaded into my soul. I could hear it and feel it. It was like a computer with all sorts of codes on it being dropped into my mind and consciousness. The partial answers and blanks were being filled in. I knew things beyond my lower self's scope and capabilities. I knew the answers to the questions about life. These were things I hadn't thought about much before that night. The portal was permanently cracked open.

My Spirit team informed me that it was time to begin the next chapter of my life that would include talking about them more and sharing information on them. This included revealing helpful guidance that can assist in improving someone else's life and well-being as well as my own. It would be to teach others these spiritual principles that were guided to me. It was time for me to use the gifts that I have in a positive way.

In a sense, after that moment I was coming out of the spiritual closet. For about ten years, I was keenly aware that I was intended to talk about them, but I put it off and made excuses. It didn't interest me enough to do that. This all changed after that night.

This was a near death experience where I had died. It was not the permanent human death that my mother dreamt of. The only thing she saw in her dream was that I died. Clairvoyant visions often need to be interpreted in order to decode the real meaning of the message that is being delivered.

A week later, my human life father passed away abruptly and without warning. Although I say, 'without warning', those close to me recall it differently. When I notified my friends of his death, they all said separately and very matter of fact, "...but you had said about six months ago that you kept getting that he would pass away suddenly this year."

They knew that I would often say things that ended up happening. This wasn't something I discussed, but it was something others would point out sporadically over the course of my life. It was never seen as unusual to them. They didn't know anything else while around me. As I moved down the new spiritual path and began teaching through the written word, then my closest friends would comment, "I'm not surprised this is who you are now, since you were always displaying hints that this is what was to come for as long as I've known you."

When I state things, I don't think too much of it until it happens, or others point it out. This is typical for channelers who receive messages. You're in an altered state of consciousness that is separate from your human physical self that it's almost like another person.

I have many different selves within me that were split apart from one self during adolescence due to the violent abusive upbringing I had. But the part of me that accesses the information is an entirely different self in a much higher space. To me, he's almost another person, which is why I rarely recall what he's said.

Near death experiences are not terribly common, but not terribly uncommon. Those who have had a near death experience will typically go through something painful and agonizing that leads them to this experience. When they revert back to human consciousness, they're not quite the same anymore. They see circumstances, life, the planet, and its people differently than they did before the death. Their senses are suddenly strengthened and they have a great understanding of their purpose preceding this moment.

The near death experience takes that soul down a different path than they were already on. It is a route they normally would not have gone down months before the experience. Nor is it something they believed they would have ever chosen to travel down a decade prior, even if they had a hunch it would lead to that. The experience shakes up the individual that alters their life course where they now know what they must do.

It's like night and day where they were working at a job they always loved, but the experience snaps them out of it and the job is abruptly no longer interesting to them. The type of friendships they once gravitated towards is also no longer an attraction to them. They see things in a more profound way. They immediately get to work and know what they must do. This clarity does not only come from a near death experience, but a spiritual transition of any kind. It is a moment in someone's life where their entire being is transformed and so is the path they're on. When they were once floundering, they're now focused.

My mother didn't immediately tell me about the dream she had about my death because it was too horrifying, but then when my father passed away a week later, she thought the dream might be connected to that. We knew that it was the metaphysical and metaphorical death of me, as I wasn't quite the same person I was prior to that night of the death.

Heaven explained the connection of moving my father out of the way and out of my life, so that I could begin the next chapter of what was to come. Although in the final years of my father's Earthly life, our relationship was healthier and more like a best friendship. It was a complete turnaround and different set up than the one I had with him while growing up. He was the one that caused my soul to fragment in adolescence. That block was present in my subconscious preventing me from getting to work on my life purpose. This is where the angels came in and disrupted my life in a challenging and welcoming way where my former selves burned into the ground. This was in order to raise me up in fire like the Phoenix rising more powerful and stronger than ever before.

Where there is Darkness there is Light. I've always lived comfortably in both worlds diving down into the depths of the darkness burning up in death only to rise out of the ashes mightier than before.

Having lived several lifetimes in one open to a wider variety of experiences than most can handle I've fragmented into dozens of selves only to merge in and out of one and back again. Sometimes you have to get beat up a bit to get a little street smart. I reside in immeasurable degrees of good and bad, light and dark, walking that fine line into both elements equally. The torment, the anguish, the joy, and the love all intertwined in an appealing cocktail every second. Being a highly tuned in sponge has its plusses and negatives depending on which direction you channel it. It makes for some interesting rock and roll.

My entire life I've been an independent lone wolf that has demanded and garnered respect since I was a teen. In High School, I was a magnet for others who would approach me needing counseling or assistance. Those from every clique would be searching the halls for me, or finding me on the bleachers to talk to me about a problem they were having. This was from the brain, the jock, the teachers, the cheerleaders, the rebels, the bully, and the bullied. When I was done with them, they would all make similar statements along the lines of, "You always know just what to say that helps me. It's like you're this old soul who is hundreds of years old, but you're just a kid in High School."

I knew from way back then who I was and what my purpose would be, such as writing the messages of God to help others improve and sharpen up their life. It is to help others become more in tune to the messages they are receiving in their own life and how to differentiate them from one of false guidance. It's teaching others how to respect themselves and those around them.

When you are tuned into your Guide and Angel, you are paying attention to your intuition. When your senses are fine tuned and highly calibrated, you become more on the mark when it comes to what is right or wrong. Your senses and feelings will tell you when something doesn't feel right. The second you feel any measure of negativity in your feelings, then trust that. Have faith in the guidance of your Guide and Angel when they tell you when something does not feel right. Follow your gut on any decisions you make in your life. Pay attention to your higher self's voice which has the most accurate answers. Take pride in who you are and what you do and set out to do. Love all that you are and avoid any negative self talk, since that is not real or aligned with Heaven.

Talk to God, Heaven and your Spirit team daily. Ask for help with anything you need assistance on. Think of the good things you have and thank your team regularly for helping you obtain that. Be grateful that you have a roof over your head, or a job that pays your bills. Your Spirit team wants to be of service and they want that connection and relationship with you. You don't have to do things alone. Sometimes as one gets comfortable in their life routine you forget to communicate and request assistance.

This asking for help can also be beyond asking your guides for help. It is also asking those around you for help or intervention in areas you feel stuck in. Stop hurting yourself and love yourself more. Don't let anybody stop you from going after what you want. You have a purpose and you are important. Ignite your inner life force that is alive and well within you screaming to get out.

They're showing me a car driving forward on the road, but there are speed bumps about every one hundred feet. The driver can drive forward, but at a slower speed than usual. If the driver puts pedal to the metal, then it'll thrash the car as it hits those speed bumps.

This is a metaphor that says move forward in life, but do it calmly, gradually, and methodically. Notice the signs on the road around you as you travel down it. Follow those signs that your Spirit team shows you. They do this not to meddle with your life, but to help guide you and bring you to a higher level of happiness. This can be working with you through a stressful time, to dissolve or reduce toxic addictions, negative connections, worry, anxiety, fears, financial issues, or rejection.

When they guide you, and you follow it and take action, then your life is more manageable, peaceful, and full of love and joy. While in that state, there is nothing you cannot do and be. In that state, you know and understand what it's like to be in Heaven. Universal change begins with each individual. All souls are here to express kindness, compassion, tolerance, and love to others. To experience love with another is to understand what God is, so love more and love often.

Stand in Your Power

The follow up to *"Ignite Your Inner Life Force"* is available in paperback and e-book by Kevin Hunter, *"Awaken Your Creative Spirit"*

Your creative spirit is present when you experience positive energy flowing through you. This energy is ignited when you make a direct connection with God. This vibration state is where you have access to the true you, which is your higher self. Your higher self rules when you work to strip, reduce, or dissolve any negative tampering influenced by a domination of your physical surroundings. Make a connection with something greater than yourself and allow that energy Light to permeate your soul and cleanse it of toxic debris. This will assist in the process of awakening your creative spirit from slumber.

Your creative spirit is more than being artistic and getting involved in creativity pursuits, although this is a good part of it. When your creative spirit is activated by a high vibration state of being, then this is the space you create from. You can apply this to your dealings in life, your creative and artistic pursuits, and to having a greater communication line with your Spirit team on the Other Side.

Your creative spirit brings your soul into a high vibration state of being because coming from a place of creativity raises your vibration. This is the place where you create and manifest your visions at higher levels while moving you into the joy of your life. It is thinking like a kid, unleashing your inner artist, and realizing your soul's potential. When you claim your celestial power with the assistance of your heavenly helpers by your side on your Earthly life, then this assists in capitalizing the true divine power within you. *Awaken Your Creative Spirit* is an overview of what it means to have access to Divine assistance and how that plays a part in arousing the muse within you in order to bring your state of mind into a happier space.

Available in paperback and e-book by Kevin Hunter, "Realm of the Wise One"

In the Spirit Worlds and the dimensions that exist, reside numerous kingdoms that house a plethora of Spirits that inhabit various forms. One of these tribes is called the Wise Ones, a darker breed in the spirit realm who often chooses to incarnate into a human body one lifetime after another for important purposes.

The *Realm of the Wise One* takes you on a magical journey to the spirit world where the Wise Ones dwell. This is followed with in-depth and detailed information on how to recognize a human soul who has incarnated from the Wise One Realm.

Author, Kevin Hunter, is a Wise One who uses the knowledge passed onto him by his Spirit team of Guides and Angels to relay the wisdom surrounding all things Wise One. He discusses the traits, purposes, gifts, roles, and personalities among other things that make up someone who is a Wise One.

Wise Ones have come in the guises of teachers, shaman, leaders, hunters, mediums, entertainers and others. *Realm of the Wise One* is an informational guide devoted to the tribe of the Wise Ones, both in human form and on the other side.

Also available in paperback and e-book by Kevin Hunter,

"Reaching for the Warrior Within"

Reaching for the Warrior Within is the author's personal story recounting a volatile childhood. This led him to a path of addictions, anxiety and overindulgence in alcohol, drugs, cigarettes and destructive relationships. As a survival mechanism, he split into many different "selves". He credits turning his life around, not by therapy, but by simultaneously paying attention to the messages he has been receiving from his Spirit team in Heaven since birth.

Kevin Hunter gains strength, healing and direction with the help of his own team of Guides and Angels. Living vicariously through this inspiring story will enable you to distinguish when you have been assisted on your own life path. *Reaching for the Warrior Within* attests that anyone can change if they pay attention to their own inner guidance system and take action. This can be from being a victim of child abuse, or a drug and alcohol user, to going after the jobs and relationships you want. This powerful story is for those seeking motivation to change, alter and empower their life one day at a time.

Available in paperback and e-book by Kevin Hunter,

"WARRIOR OF LIGHT
Messages from my Guides and Angels"

There are legions of angels, spirit guides, and departed loved ones in heaven that watch and guide you on your journey here on Earth. They are around to make your life easier and less stressful. Do you pay attention to the nudges, guidance, and messages given to you? There are many who live lives full of negativity and stress while trying to make ends meet. This can shake your faith as it leads you down paths of addictions, unhealthy life choices, and negative relationship connections. Learn how you can recognize the guidance of your own Spirit team of Guides and Angels around you.

Author, Kevin Hunter, relays heavenly guided messages about getting humanity, the world, and yourself into shape. He delivers the guidance passed onto him by his own Spirit team on how to fine tune your body, soul and raise your vibration. Doing this can help you gain hope and faith in your own life in order to start attracting in more abundance.

Available in paperback and e-book by Kevin Hunter,

"Empowering Spirit Wisdom
A Warrior of Light's Guide on Love, Career and the Spirit World"

Kevin Hunter relays heavenly, guided messages for everyday life concerns with his book, *Empowering Spirit Wisdom*. Some of the topics covered are your soul, spirit and the power of the light, laws of attraction, finding meaningful work, transforming your professional and personal life, navigating through the various stages of dating and love relationships, as well as other practical affirmations and messages from the Archangels. Kevin Hunter passes on the sensible wisdom given to him by his own Spirit team in this inspirational book.

Available in paperback and e-book by Kevin Hunter,
"Darkness of Ego"

The biggest cause of turmoil and conflict in one's life is executed by the human ego. All souls have an ego. The most unruly and destructive ego exists within every human soul. When the soul enters into a physical human body, the ego immediately compresses and then swells up. It is the higher self's goal to ensure that it remains in check while living an Earthly life.

The ego is what tests each soul along its journey. It is how one learns right from wrong. The experiences and challenges that the soul has while living in this Earthly life school contribute to the soul's growth. When a soul learns lessons, it is intended and expected to grow and enhance from the experience. Yet, there are a great many souls who do not learn lessons and remain in the same spot. The ill of the bunch wreaks all kinds of havoc, destruction, judgment and heart ache in its wake.

In *Darkness of Ego*, author Kevin Hunter infuses some of the guidance, messages, and wisdom he's received from his Spirit team surrounding all things ego related. The ego is one of the most damaging culprits in human life. Therefore it is essential to understand the nature of the beast in order to navigate gracefully out of it when it spins out of control. Some of the topics covered in *Darkness of Ego* are humanity's destruction, mass hysteria, karmic debt, and the power of the mind, heaven's gate, the ego's war on love and relationships, and much more.

Available in paperback and e-book by Kevin Hunter, "The Seven Deadly Sins"

The Seven Deadly Sins is a mini-pocket book that takes a look at the traditional sins in a practical way. The Seven Deadly Sins in today's language would be the Seven Toxic Challenges. Being aware of these toxic challenges are helpful since falling into a deadly sin creates a block from achieving greatness, finding peace, and picking up on the messages and guidance coming in from Heaven. The messages and guidance are intended to help guide you along your path. You were born with an ego that expands as it enters the Earth's atmosphere. This ego causes you to struggle and have conflicts as it attempts to take over you and dominate your actions, thoughts, and feelings. When your ego runs recklessly it grows and expands into darkness. The dark ego is what prompts you to wrestle with challenges in this lifetime. These challenges were called *sin* during ancient times. The sins committed can delay you on your path and wreak havoc on your soul's innate system. This innate system is the higher self part of you that governs your life through a broader perspective.

The seven deadly sins were created in order to assist human souls in making sounder choices. They are challenges that all human souls wrestle with to one degree or another. When you're deeply absorbed in these toxic challenges, then it causes an array of issues and complications on your life path. These sins or challenges prevent the positive flow of energy and abundance in your life. They also play a hand at creating a block that stops up the communication line with your team on the Other Side. The sins or toxic challenges looked at include, Pride, Envy, Greed, Lust, Gluttony, Wrath and Sloth.

The *Warrior of Light* series of pocket books are available in paperback and e-book by Kevin Hunter called, *Spirit Guides and Angels, Soul Mates and Twin Flames, Divine Messages for Humanity, Raising Your Vibration, Connecting with the Archangels*

About KEVIN HUNTER

Kevin Hunter is an author, love expert and channeler. His books tackle a variety of genres and tend to have a strong male protagonist. The messages and themes he weaves in his work surround Spirit's own communications of love and respect, which he channels and infuses into his writing and stories.

His books include the Warrior of Light series of books, *Warrior of Light: Messages from my Guides and Angels, Realm of the Wise One, Empowering Spirit Wisdom, Reaching for the Warrior Within, Darkness of Ego, Ignite Your Inner Life Force, Awaken Your Creative Spirit,* and *The Seven Deadly Sins.* He is also the author of the horror, drama, *Paint the Silence,* and the modern day erotic love story, *Jagger's Revolution.*

Before writing books and stories, Kevin started out in the entertainment business in 1996 becoming actress Michelle Pfeiffer's personal development dude for her boutique production company, Via Rosa Productions. She dissolved her company after several years and he made a move into coordinating film productions for the big studios on such films as *One Fine Day, A Thousand Acres, The Deep End of the Ocean, Crazy in Alabama, Original Sin, The Perfect Storm, Harry Potter & the Sorcerer's Stone, Dr. Dolittle 2* and *Carolina.* He considers himself a love addict and beach bum born and raised in Los Angeles, California.

Visit www.kevin-hunter.com